THE RESID

THE RESIDUE REPORT

THE ACTION PLAN FOR SAFER FOOD

Stephanie Lashford

THORSONS PUBLISHING GROUP

First published 1988

Illustrated by Ian Dicks

British Library Cataloguing in Publication Data

Lashford, Stephanie
   The residue report: the action plan for
   safer food.
   1. Food. Contaminants. Residues
   I. Title
   363.1'92

   ISBN 0-7225-1481-6

Published by Thorsons Publishers Limited,
Wellingborough, Northamptonshire, NN8 2RQ, England

Printed in Great Britain by Biddles Limited, Guildford, Surrey

10 9 8 7 6 5 4 3

Contents

This book is dedicated to my parents

Acknowledgements

Mary Campbell: a big thank you for our continual close working relationship, which I have appreciated immensely. The far reaching effects of this report would not have been possible without your help and assistance. Margaret Foster: a big thank you also for your continual support and the contributions made that have enhanced the depth of certain areas of this book, and for your much appreciated efforts in typing the manuscript.

I would also like to thank the following in alphabetical order for contributing their ideas and knowledge to this book. The material for this report is diverse and far reaching – we have uncovered the connections between seemingly unrelated events. We have tried to show the true implications of the effects of residues in our environment. We can only begin to understand the real problems in our environment once the findings of this report become common knowledge and people begin to act upon the information. It is only a beginning for others to consider, follow and use to bring about change.

Paddy Ashdown (leader of the SLD); Stuart Ashley (Cardiff Friends of the Earth); Dr A. Barbeau (deceased — Etiology of Parkinson's Disease, Montreal, Canada); Donald Barltrop (Consultant in Child Health, Westminster Hospital, London); Mrs Belinda Barnes; Barry Bessant (Alzheimer's Disease Society, St Mellons, Cardiff); Francis Blake (Soil Association); Martin Conyers (Cardiff City Farm); Peter Durr; Professor J. A. Edwardson (MRC Neuroendocrinological Unit, Newcastle General Hospital); Alan Gear (Executive Director, Henry Doubleday Research Association); T. J. Horsefield (National Farmers' Union); Dr J. W. Langston (currently researching into MPTP and Parkinson's Disease, Montreal, Canada); Jack Levenson; Philip

Lockwood (Branch Development Director, Parkinson's Disease Society); Sanford P. Markey (National Institute of Health, Bethesda U.S.A.); David Powell; Mark Purdey (Farmer); Jenny Randerson (Liberal Councillor, Cardiff); the T.U.C.; Helen Woodley (Permaculture Association).

Foreword

The consumer is under attack from many quarters. This excellent book by Stephanie Lashford makes plain that it is time for consumers to unite in their own defence. Earlier this year, Consumer Watch was set up for this purpose; and we were delighted to appoint Mrs Lashford as head of our research unit. We are even more delighted that she has written this book.

So often we are warned of dangers; so seldom told how to avert them. This book does both. Those powerful forces that are ranged against the consumer will either ignore the warnings it contains and persuade their apologists in the media and public offices to do the same, or they will dismiss the charges as exaggerated or emotive, but I defy them to do either. Mrs Lashford has written a book too important to be ignored and too well-researched and too full of fact to be dismissed as either exaggerated or emotive.

She has left me with two points to make. The protectionist food lobby is never still for a moment, for they are never short of ideas to advance their own interests at the expense of the consumer, and almost always they ask for another limit to be placed upon the consumers' freedom of choice.

As I write this, it is reported that the Dairy Trade Federation is asking the UK Government and the EEC Commission to propose a further cut in the quantity of butter the British people will be allowed to buy from New Zealand. Were it not for the high tax that has to be paid on butter imported from New Zealand, it would be half the price it is. That is bad enough, but what is really much worse is that New Zealand farmers, having the climate to produce dairy products at a lower cost than any other country in the world, are not induced to use nitrates, hormones and antibiotics as others do. Their butter, so some doctors tell us, is less likely to have a harmful effect upon our health.

When it comes to food, the British people ought to make two claims, it seems. They should have the freedom to choose what they would like to buy, without a tax or prohibition being placed upon it to deflect their choice. That freedom they most certainly have not got now. Secondly, they should have available to them information to judge the safety of their food, and that is something this book goes a long way towards doing.

That brings us to the second point. The link between food and health is, to most of us, rather obvious. The wrong kind of food – the polluted and adulterated – has an extra cost that we may pay long after it is purchased and eaten, and that cost we pass on to the National Health Service. The Ministry of Food is fused with Agriculture and Fisheries, certainly to the detriment of the consumer and taxpayer, while Health, now so rightly separated from Social Security is in a better position than ever before to help the consumer. This book provides plenty of evidence from which to infer the need for a new ministry, the Department of Food and Health. Those who worry about the rising cost of the health service would then have an active interest in getting to the cause of ill health.

May this book be widely read and may millions heed its warnings and act upon its advice.

SIR RICHARD BODY,
Chairman of Consumer Watch, Former Chairman of the House of Commons Select Committee on Agriculture

Preface

What are residues? What have they to do with me?

Literally defined, residues means 'little bits left behind' – a small word for such a vast array of different materials. This book's intention is to change your whole concept of the word. By the final page it is hoped that you will see that its meaning has a great deal to do with you.

The residues which we are going to look at are the parts of your daily food that are not proteins, fat, vitamins, mineral salts, fibre, food additives or water but those chemical materials that have become part of your daily diet because of the way food has been grown or produced. You are likely to be totally unaware of these residues.

My hope is that this book will not just highlight the dangers of food contamination but will be the spur to bring about real change.

We live in a world that is far from satisfactory as regards food cultivation and production but there are positive and viable alternatives. I hope *The Residue Report* will stimulate the same concern and enthusiasm for the subject that the consumer developed for food additives. As soon as you discovered that additives were possibly carcinogenic and allergenic and caused hyperactivity and other behavioural problems you voted with your supermarket trolley and we now have an ever-increasing range of additive-free products.

We don't need legislation to ban pesticides or stop the misuse and abuse of growth promoters and antibiotics in animal rearing. You the consumer must make it known what you are willing to buy, and by the time you have seen the evidence for removing pesticides and growth promoters you will only want to buy organic fruit and vegetables and cereals and residue-reduced meat and fish and poultry. Then we shall see the growth of a new industry – an honest, wholesome food industry.

Introduction

As we have changed from an agricultural and rural society to an industrialized and urbanized one we have lost our empathy with the land upon which our existence depends, and greed has come to play a major part in our production and choice of food. Wants and needs have changed, and consumers have come to expect perfect, blemish-free foods at low prices. They expect year-round availability with no change in flavour, texture or price. They do not expect to buy any substandard goods unless they are considerably cheaper: it is acceptable to buy vegetables past their best at a knock-down price. Consumers would not generally accept, if asked, that they were being greedy, but simply trying to get the best value for money. Their attitudes to food are reinforced by the advertising industry.

Millions of pounds are spent on 'image-building', and then consumers work as hard as is humanly possible to copy and imitate these images. Advertising campaigns are meticulously thought out and use psychological tactics to play on people's inhibitions. They home in on certain groups such as children, busy working mothers and young, inexperienced mothers, and try to sell them products which they imply will increase and improve their standing and prestige amongst their friends and acquaintances.

TV adverts have become an essential ingredient in the launching of a new product, making it difficult for truly beneficial products to make an impact on the market. In 1985 the food industry spent £325.4 million on advertising and a further £2,400 million on packaging.

Food accounts for 15 per cent of all advertising, making it the single biggest sector. Chocolate and ready-to-eat breakfast cereals, when put together, represent nearly one quarter of the total spent on food advertising. Products with the poorest nutritional benefits, those foods that we could do well to stop eating altogether, have the most spent on them. For example, it was only necessary to spend £3 million on promoting fresh fruit and vegetables, but since the 'You are what you eat' campaign people now consume considerably more fresh fruit and vegetables, realizing the obvious benefits.

Supermarkets often claim that they are responding to the wants of consumers by providing blemish-free, uniform sized, cleaned and packaged foods and by continually changing lines and convenience foods (designer foods). In fact there seems to be little advice available as to what the wants of the customer really are. Although we have seen the introduction of nutritional information sheets and labels displayed in supermarkets, and an increase in the range of 'health' products, these should only be the beginning of a real change.

It is not clear how much of supermarket profits is actually spent on research and development. As with other industries we should expect companies to pay for independent analysis of products, look at improved production techniques (e.g. organic growing methods), study the individual nutritional needs of the consumer and look at the pesticide and drug contents of all food. This type of service is not yet available but as the consumer's awareness of foods and the relationship between food and health grows, it must become standard supermarket practice.

Supermarkets should also consider promoting more specialist lines that reflect 'true' health foods and minority tastes. Some of these individual areas of concern could even be used as advertising features as part of a customer service that may even improve profits!

If you were to ask a supermarket, for example: what pesticide sprays are left on your cornflakes? or can you be one hundred per cent certain that your growers allow the necessary number of days between spraying and harvesting? the responses tend to be either unco-operative or else bending over backwards to give you as much information as possible. You will be able to work out from their information policies which supermarkets are the most concerned.

The time has come for the enormous supermarket profits to be examined and more questions asked. Are they making too much money out of us? Should our food be cheaper? Should we not be expecting rather more for our money? Major companies should be made to help pay for research into heart disease, diabetes, dietary disorders and other food-related illnesses. In-store nutritionists should offer impartial advice on health and diet.

Supermarkets enter into contracts to take the produce grown by a particular grower, providing certain criteria are met. They negotiate quality and price and the deal is set. By entering into this contract some farmers may be forced into operating in accordance with standards set down by a company manager rather than by their own natural skills and judgement.

Nevertheless, many farmers consider the use of agro-chemicals as a positive move away from back-breaking labour, lower yields and time-consuming methods. Who can blame farmers and growers for wanting to escape from long hours and hard work? A combination of new mechanical technology, more reliable and efficient machinery and sound organic principles could be the way forward to reducing the residue content of our foods.

The pressure to adopt a certain style of farming is great, for EEC subsidies and grants are only given to those supporting an agro-chemical farming system, and growing certain produce. The farmer and grower is faced at present with an almost impossible situation. Does he do without an assured supply of money and go it alone (as many organic producers do) or does he go along with the system and be financially rewarded for following EEC policies? The latter also has its drawbacks. The farmer's present position is not as secure as he once thought, as surpluses have caused changes in EEC policies, leaving him very vulnerable. But, if he does make a break and go organic, he will have assured outlets for his produce as Safeways are offering contracts for those willing to comply with Soil Association standards for organic products.

A powerful force for the status quo is the chemical industry. These giant companies exist to make a profit, and their marketing divisions exist to develop products to sell to the agricultural industry. But sales reps and marketing people should not take the blame. When one is involved in the selling of a certain product one can become blind to its shortcomings. When you are told that the research figures should be 'sensibly interpreted' and that exposure to certain chemicals is of minimal risk an employee with limited scientific knowledge has little opportunity to voice concern. Persistent querying or questioning could ruin job prospects.

Image is important to chemical companies. They like to be seen
as creating a good future for the country, offering help and advice
and showing environmental concern. Consumers must assess the
truth of this imagery for themselves.

The agro-chemical industry is trying to become the crutch on
which many farmers lean, especially as intensive farming has in
recent times been actively encouraged. However, with the acute
embarrassment of the surpluses still on the faces of government
ministers, the time has come for change.

Three important questions should be asked: What does the
customer intend to do with the chemicals? How does the customer
intend to dispose of waste such as containers, leftover materials
etc.? In the event of contamination, what should the customer do?

Chemical companies should offer back-up services and be held
entirely responsible for misuse and abuse. The principle of 'the
polluter pays' should be strictly upheld. The consumer has the
right to expect this of professional chemists, as many people simply
do not have the expertise or knowledge to recognize any potential
hazards. The record of the chemical industry does not inspire
confidence. Court proceedings can mean the financial ruination
of a consumer, and so proceedings are never brought. The legal
machinery seems to be weighted against the individual.

The chemical giants use advertising techniques which border
on the subversive. One advertisement in the national press portrayed
a loaf of bread that 'would cost in excess of £3, should chemicals
stop being applied to the ground'. The inference is that without
your 'friendly chemical giants' your food would cost far more. This
implied that organic methods of production were expensive,
unreliable and prone to pests and diseases. Such insinuations are
completely unfounded.

Since consumers are going to want residue-reduced foods in the
same way as they now expect additive-free foods, the 'chemical
giants' should be changing their emphasis, looking into organic
farming methods and coming up with new product lines in this
area. The need for reliable organic materials to aid the organic farmer,
grower and gardener is already there. Companies must come to
terms with the fact that once people associate ill health with
exposure to food residues, their role must change. One of the biggest
British pesticide manufacturers (fifth biggest in the world) is ICI.
In a good year, its profits are in excess of £1 billion. Approximately

one-third of these profits come from sales of drugs and pesticides.

There is little hope of change being initiated by the Government. It makes changes only in areas that benefit its monetarist policies, not in health, conservation or ecology.

The usual method of looking into large scale health problems such as heart disease is to set up a working party. Reports are often written up during the research period. These interim reports provide an outline of the problem and a general idea of the work being carried out. When the research is complete, the reports are written up in full and then *in theory* released to the general public. Often, however, drafts of reports are sent back to the working parties with a suggestion that they be 'toned down'.

Those who bring public attention to ecological matters are sometimes referred to as pressure groups. Their ultimate effectiveness suffers from possibly biased press reports, financial restrictions, fragmentation and a lack of effective publicity machinery. They depend on volunteers, who often have other demands on their time and energies, to spread their message.

In the light of Chernobyl and such ecological issues as acid rain, these groups must put themselves on a more professional footing to ensure that their views are treated with respect and attention by the Government.

Finally, consumers and ecology groups must demand that the EEC find practical ways in which to share its food surplus with others, including the Third World. While millions die from starvation we in the West have been systematically destroying *every minute of every day*:

19 lbs of tomatoes,
41 lbs of cauliflowers,
134 lbs of apples,
1,579 lbs of peaches and
5,266 lbs of oranges.

To be able to state that there are no longer any food mountains, the EEC has seen fit to sell the surpluses to the Russians – at bargain prices:

butter at 7 pence per 455g (1 lb)
wheat at £20 per ton and
wine at 7 pence per litre (1¾ pints).

The issue of residues will be the next consumer topic to take the world by storm. With the emotions and concerns that will inevitably be aroused, we can look forward to profound changes in the production, manufacture, marketing and selling of food. These changes will begin with us, the consumers.

CHAPTER 1

Facts and figures – *pesticides*

Most consumers have cracked the E numbers code. With the following information you will be able to crack the pesticide puzzle and recognize a potentially hazardous product.

A pesticide found as a residue in food can be one of three types of chemicals:

- An insecticide
  Used to kill a wide variety, or a specific type, of insect.

- A herbicide
  Used to kill or suppress the growth of all, or certain types, of plants.

- A fungicide
  Used to kill or suppress the growth of all or of certain fungi.

In addition fumigants can be mixed with either insecticides or fungicides. They are used in a variety of situations e.g. in the sterilization of grain houses to prevent mould growth.

Insecticides

There are four main groups of insecticides: organophosphorus, organochlorides, carbamates and pyrethroids.

They can be used by the consumer or the farmer in a number

of ways. Examples are given to make identification on packets and labels easier.

Organophosphorus substances (OPs)

OPs were developed to provide an alternative to the very poisonous pesticide nicotine which was a very widely used chemical before World War II. Organophosphorus compounds are in fact nerve gases but today they are more commonly used in diluted and modified forms as pesticides. They work on the principle of attacking the central nervous system of insects and animals.

OPs prevent the enzyme acetylcholinesterase from regulating the acetylcholine at the nerve endings. This results in an excessive build-up of the acetylcholine.

Contact: The chemical is put in direct contact with the pest and can be used as a spray or a powder. One application will only kill those it directly touches – it does not have a lasting effect. *Example*: Mevinphos.

Persistent Contact: This means that the chemical is put in direct contact with the pest as a spray or a powder and is effective for some time after application. *Examples*: Malathion and Diazinon.

Systemic compounds: These are chemicals that are absorbed by the plants, then eaten by the insects, thus destroying them. *Example*: Dimethoate.

High vapour pressure: These are chemicals that are used as fumigants. *Example*: Dichlorvos.

Soil Application: These are chemicals that are applied directly on to the soil to destroy pests living on or in the soil, e.g., carrot fly, wire worm. *Example*: Chlorfenvinphos.

Surface application or systemic action: These are chemicals used to control small animals e.g., field mice. The substance is either eaten by or sprayed onto the pest. *Examples*: Fenchorphos and Dimethoate.

Organochlorine substances (OCs)

OCs were initially heralded as almost perfect insecticides because they were cheap, effective and *apparently* safe to humans. DDT, a member of the organochlorine group, was once used very successfully to control the insects that spread malaria, river blindness and yellow fever. However, after continued use the insects developed resistance to it so that DDT became less effective although its use still continues today.

Organochlorines are persistent pesticides. This means that the chemicals are not readily broken down into their component parts and remain active in the environment long after they have completed the task they were initially used for. This is a problem because they permeate through the food chain to animals and man. Organochlorines are lipophilic which means that they are attracted to fatty substances to be found in milk, cheese, meat, human fat and breast milk. It is the accumulation of these fat soluble OCs that is of concern (see page 100, for further details).

There are three main types of OCs:-

DDT related substances (*Example*: Methoxyechlor);

BHC Lindane and related chemicals (see page 29)

Aldrin and related chemicals (see page 27)

Carbamates

These are naturally occurring substances that have their place in medicine and are used to treat glaucoma, epilepsy and neuralgia. From investigations carried out for their use as medicines, it was discovered that they could also be used as effective insecticides. During this research several thousands were tested, but at present only 20 have been marketed as insecticides.

Carbamates work as insecticides on the same principle as OPs. They are twice as expensive as other insecticides and used only when all else has failed. *Examples*: Carbaryl, Carbofuran and Aldicarb (see table on page 27 for details).

Pyrethroids

There are two main types of pyrethroids:

Natural: from the flower of the chrysanthemum family

Synthetic: the first synthetic pyrethroid was Allethrin (see table) on page 27) developed in 1949. Since then many more synthetic pyrethroids have been marketed and their use has dramatically increased in recent years. They are readily broken down into non toxic-chemicals but will kill bees and are toxic to fish.

Herbicides

Herbicides are used to remove weeds that would otherwise compete with crops for the nutrients in the soil and the light. They can be divided into two groups: selective and non selective.

Selective herbicides destroy a particular weed without damaging the crop.

Non selective herbicides give total weed control for the maximum time possible, e.g. those used to keep garden paths weed free. These herbicides are intended to kill *all* types of plants.

Herbicides are generally applied in one of three following ways:

Foliar application

Systemic

The herbicide is applied to the leaves and foliage of the weeds and is absorbed into the plant. *Examples*: 2.4.5-T, Paraquat, Aminotriazole (see table for details, page 27)

Contact herbicides

These chemicals are applied to the foliage and it is only the treated areas of the plant which will die. Examples are: Dinoseb and Ioxynil.

Soil application

These chemicals are applied to the soil between ploughing and sowing to keep a weed-free environment and allow seedlings to flourish. This also means that the farmer does not have to mechanically weed the field during the growing season. *Example*: Di-allate (see table for details, page 29).

Most herbicides work by either:

Interfering with the photosynthesis of the plant, thereby preventing growth;

accelerating growth-producing 'bolting' and eventual dying or interfering with the fat metabolism of the plant.

Fungicides

Fungicides are used to prevent fungal growth and for the treatment of established fungal infection of perishable foodstuffs i.e. animal feed, grain and flour. Fungicides can be divided into three groups:

Heavy metals and inorganic

Non systemic are most effective when applied before infection sets in. This is because they are persistent and their effectiveness lasts for a long time. This is of interest to the consumer because the fungicide can become a food residue (the health risks attached to these chemicals are discussed on page 44). *Examples*: Maneb, Thiram, Ziram, Captan, Captafol, Pentachlorophenol.

Systemic are most effective against the fungus once it is visible. Fungi are well able to mutate thereby developing resistance to chemicals which can result in excessive amounts being applied and therefore increasing possible food residues. *Examples*: there are seven groups of systemic fungicides but the type most commonly found as food residues are the benzimidazoles e.g. Benomyl (see table for details, page 28).

In 1985 it was found that lemons being sold on the British market had excessive residues of Thiabendazole (a member of the benzimidazole group of fungicides) in their skins. This compound is mainly used in Britain to protect stored potatoes.

Miscellaneous pesticides

We have covered the major groups of pesticides. The following do not fall neatly into the main categories:

Ectoparasiticides: chemicals that destroy ticks and mites found on the skin/fur of animals, e.g., sheep dip.

Herbicide and fertilizer mix: a combination preparation which is used to kill off weeds and make the desired crop grow, e.g., lawn improvers.

Seed treatments: a combination preparation which ensures that the seeds do not deteriorate in storage. The treated seeds are often sold in foil packages to prevent premature germination and to increase shelf life. Treated seeds intended for growing must not be eaten as they are poisonous. Always check that any you buy for use in cooking are clearly labelled for culinary use.

Molluscicides: chemicals used to kill a wide variety, or a specific type of mollusc, e.g., slugs and snails.

Nematodacide: chemicals used to kill worms, e.g., used in the growing of turf.

Aphicide: chemical insecticide with specific task of killing aphids, e.g., greenfly.

Looking at selected pesticides

KEY

H   Herbicide

I   Insecticide

F   Fungicide

LD 50   Is a test scientists use to find out how poisonous a substance is. LD stands for lethal dose. For example an LD 50 of 5 means that for a group of animals weighing one kilo fed 5 mgs of a test substance half of these animals in the group will die (50%). The lower the LD 50 number is, the more poisonous a substance.

Definition

Carcinogen: Causes cancer. Tests are performed on animals, usually rats or mice, and so it is not possible to state whether it will definitely cause cancer in man. Only man's further exposure will identify the problem: as more people die from cancer enough research will eventually be carried out to establish the true facts. Until such time as positive proof is established potentially hazardous substances will still be used.

KEY (cont)

Mutagen: Causes changes in genes that may or may not cause abnormalities in further generations.

Teratogen: Interferes with the normal development of a foetus such that deformed offspring can be born.

Allergen: A substance that causes some type of reaction in people when they are exposed to it, e.g., a hypersensitive state.

* * *   These substances have been highlighted because of their widespread use. This means that their presence presents more occasions when man could become contaminated either through residues left in or on food, direct contact or by human error or abuse.

Name	Function	How used	Where found	Approx. Oral LD	Possible side effects
Aldrin	I	*As a dust or a liquid*	Used as a seed dressing and animal dip. Used on wire worms in potatoes. Used on compost. Restricted in Britain and 7 other countries. Banned in 9 other countries.	10	Carcinogen Teratogen Mutagen Allergen
Allethrin	I	*Used as a fly and wasp spray for household use.*	Unsuitable to be used near fish.	10	Mutagen Allergen
Aminotriazole (Amitrole)	H	*Systemic through the roots and foliage*	Controls docks, many grasses and other broadleaved weeds. Used prior to sowing, ploughed into the ground to act as a slow releasing herbicide. Also used on rape. In certain conditions must wait 6 weeks before sowing. Used in orchards. Restricted in Sweden. Banned in Norway.	11,000	Carcinogen Teratogen Mutagen Irritant to eyes, skin, lungs.

Name	Function	How used	Where found	Approx. Oral LD	Possible side effects
Benomyl	F	*Systemic*	Widely used on fruit. Kills spiders and mites. Banned in Finland. Remains in the soil for up to 6 months.	More than 10,000	Carcinogen Teratogen Mutagen Allergen
Captafol (Difolatan) *See also* **Captan**	F	*Non-systemic*	Expensive so used very little. Used for potato blight.	2,500	Carcinogen Teratogen Mutagen Allergen
Captan	F	*Non-systemic*	Used as a seed treatment. Very persistent. Taints foods and is therefore a detectable residue by distinctive taste. Harmful to fish. Banned in Norway.	10	Carcinogen Teratogen Mutagen Allergen Irritant to skin, eyes, lungs.
Carbaryl	I	*As a contact on leaves*	Used as a selective herbicide on apple trees to ensure large fruit by killing off a percentage of the fertilized blossom (growth regulator). Kills worms, earwigs, caterpillars. Recommended interval one week. *Very widely* used – short persistence.	850	Carcinogen Teratogen Mutagen Absorbed through the skin.
Carbon Tetrachloride	Fumigant	*Spray*	Added to other fumigants to make them less flammable. Used largely on grain. One week interval.	2,800	A liver and kidney poison. Carcinogen Teratogen Allergen
Chlordane (Organo Chlorine)	I	*Spray*	Has a limited use only. For use on turf to kill worms. Essential to keep animals away for 2 weeks from treated area. Banned in 5 countries. Severely restricted in 9.	457	Carcinogen Teratogen Mutagen

Name	Function	How used	Where found	Approx. Oral LD	Possible side effects
Di-allate	H	*Used on the soil*	Used prior to sowing to act as a slow releasing herbicide. Used on sugar beet and animal fodder e.g., mangolds, cauliflower, swede and turnip and generally all the brassica family. Very persistent. (Not approved product 1985.)	395	Carcinogen Mutagen Allergen
Dichlorvos • • •	I	*As a vapour, powder/dust.* *Very important as used extensively in the home*	Used for spraying houseflies and wasps, and fleas etc. usually onto animals. Used also in greenhouses and mushroom houses. A 'part 3' poison – this means full protective clothing must be used.	46	Carcinogen Teratogen Mutagen Allergen
Dieldrin	I	*Spray*	A cattle dip. Once used as a treatment for wood-worm in houses! Persistent. Banned 13 countries. Restricted in 6.	46	Carcinogen Teratogen Mutagen Allergen Avoid skin contact as absorbed through the skin.
Ethylene oxide	Fumigant		Used on stored grain. Banned in New Zealand. Restricted in West Germany.	72	Carcinogen Teratogen Mutagen Allergen
Formaldehyde (As a gas)		*As a soil disinfectant. There should be an interval of up to 6 weeks after use*	Controls foot rot in sheep.	260	Carcinogen Mutagen Allergen
As a solution is known as **Formalayn**		*As an additive in the making of silage*	Used as a preservative in some hair shampoos. Also used in the preservation of biological animal specimens.		A general irritant.
Lindane (BHC, CHC) Not approved	I	*Spray* *It is used as a seed dressing, the*	Used as a fumigant in greenhouses for insects.	40	Carcinogen Tetratogen Allergen

Name	Function	How used	Where found	Approx. Oral LD	Possible side effects
		products grown from these seeds must not be used for human consumption	Bees and fish must be kept away for 2 weeks. Banned in 4 countries. Severely restricted in 7.		
Maneb • • • Widely used so side effects are significant	F	*Non-systemic*	Used for potato blight and mildew. Should be an interval of up to 7 days between application and harvesting. Banned in USSR. Restricted in Canada.	6,750	Carcinogen Teratogen Allergen Irritant to skin, eyes and lungs. Has deforming effects on pregnant female rats' offspring.
Nicotine	Aphicide		Used as a general spray product in the times before agro-chemicals were developed. Harmful to bees, fish and wild birds.	24	Carcinogen Teratogen Mutagen
Trichlorfon Organo phosphate	I		Used on straw and on the brassica family in general. Harmful to fish.	560	Carcinogen Teratogen Mutagen
Zineb Zinc ethylenebis dithiocarbamate • • • Most important fungicide as it is so widely used. Similar to Maneb.	F		Similar in usage to Maneb. Used for potato blight. There should be an interval of up to 3 weeks after use.	5,200	Carcinogen Teratogen Allergen Irritant to both skin and eyes.
Ziram (Not approved)	F	*Non-systemic*		1,400	Carcinogen Mutagen Allergen

Pesticides are present throughout the environment and all of us to some extent are affected by them. Each person has a different level of tolerance and sensitivity; what may be toxic to one person may not affect another at all. 'Safe' levels have never been defined by the medical profession, nor have there ever been any satisfactory studies carried out to identify those most at risk from pesticide residues. It is difficult to obtain satisfactory information as vested

Present usage in Britain

Amount spent on pesticides in Britain in 1984

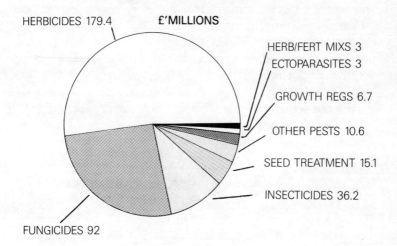

HERBICIDES 179.4   £'MILLIONS

HERB/FERT MIXS 3
ECTOPARASITES 3

GROWTH REGS 6.7

OTHER PESTS 10.6

SEED TREATMENT 15.1

INSECTICIDES 36.2

FUNGICIDES 92

TOTAL VALUE £346 MILLIONS

interests will challenge any data released. As with pesticides, the health hazards associated with smoking have long been documented, but successive governments have avoided making smoking a political issue, partly because of the financial loss in tax to the treasury should the smoking of cigarettes completely disappear. Profit, jobs and big business take an overriding preference to health.

If your house is burgled you dial 999 and the police will take over the situation and assist you. If, however, you are exposed to a potentially poisonous chemical what do you do? There are only a handful of poisons units dotted around the country where specialist help is available. Today the consumer can buy and use a wide variety of potentially lethal chemicals. So little is generally known about them that if they are used incorrectly, the consumer can become extremely vulnerable. As more products in everyday use include potentially dangerous and lethal chemicals the medical profession must be educated in recognizing their poisoning effects particularly for long term low level exposure.

If you are accidentally sprayed with a pesticide you should collect the evidence of who did it and what pesticide was used. You should then contact the Health and Safety Executive Council, Environmental Health Officers and the Civil Aviation Authority in cases of aerial spraying. However, after all this has been done the consumer should not expect a completely satisfactory result. No case can be brought in law unless negligence can be proved, meaning that the pesticide user would have had to have been spraying with an unapproved chemical and have been using it in a negligent way.

Although the law requires that 24 hours' notice should be given before aerial spraying takes place the practicalities of doing this make a nonsense of the law. Present laws have not kept pace with increasing risks to the consumer and total revision of the law in this area is long overdue.

Acute poisoning effects

The definition of acute poisoning is ingestion, inhalation or absorption by accidental encounter, direct spraying or in the manufacture of a high dose of pesticides, which leads to almost immediate symptoms of poisoning.

Industrial accidents

The most recent major accident was in Bhopal (India) when faulty valve equipment led to the release of a cloud of toxic chemicals which instantly killed those in the immediate area while they slept. After the cloud dispersed some survivors experienced breathing difficulties, blindness temporary and permanent, others nausea, vomiting and skin irritation. Normally large chemical factories pose little or no threat to the public. It is only when a series of human errors occur or when safety procedures are not strictly adhered to that catastrophes occur.

Environmental hazards

The farmer does not intend to harm the public by purposely spraying them, but if you happen to be in the wrong place at the wrong time or if the wind is in a certain direction you may be exposed to harmful chemicals that could have far-reaching consequences. A document of complaint obtained from the Agricultural Inspectorate describes an incident in 1985 when schoolchildren became ill after a cloud of spray being used on a nearby wheat field drifted through the windows of their school at the village of Bulphan near Basildon, Essex. Many of the children developed sore eyes, headaches and were gasping for breath. The Agricultural Inspectorate concluced that it was likely that they were poisoned by a mixture of three pesticides including Captafol.

On August 1 two boys aged 13 and 9 were playing in their garden at West Wickham, Cambridgeshire with a friend. All three boys were showered in pesticide from a tractor in the next field. Their mother saw the event and immediately washed off as much of the pesticide as she could. The farmer could be said to be negligent as he sprayed his field on a very windy day. The mother has taken legal advice as symptoms due to this exposure may be delayed and occur in later life. The pesticide in this particular incident was Dicquat which can cause kidney failure and liver damage.

Other confirmed cases in the document show that a pensioner was 'overcome' by a hazardous spray while working in her garden; another 'became ill' after being sprayed without warning from a helicopter; and seven golfers were sprayed by Triadmefon and Captafol from an aircraft. An 84-year-old woman cyclist had to spend two days in hospital after being drenched from a helicopter.

The document shows that more than 327 people were involved in 230 incidents investigated by that Agricultural Inspectorate but less than half the incidents were 'officially confirmed' partly because the inspectors arrived *too late* to gather all the evidence. These are the figures for reported spraying. There must be many more that are never recorded.

Allergenic effects

The process of attributing reaction (allergy) to chemicals/pesticides has been difficult to achieve. The medical profession is reluctant to link anything environmental to ill health as this could lead to demands for clearing up the environment. The science of allergy is relatively new and so clinical techniques for finding the offending chemical are still in their infancy.

American scientists are more advanced in their knowledge of the causes of allergies, and if you suspect an illness to be due to exposure to a pesticide a sample of your blood could be flown to a laboratory in Texas for analysis. In this country, the most forward-thinking clinic is that run by Dr Jean Munro (see page 50 for details).

Allergic reactions are as individual as fingerprints. Not all people react adversely to pesticides (chemicals) but there are several thousands of different chemicals in our environment and as many potentially different types of allergic reactions. Making the task of identifying the chemical culprit even more difficult is the 'cocktail effect': an individual chemical will behave in a certain way when mixed with other chemicals and quite differently when it is on its own. The fact that there are several thousand pesticides/chemicals in use makes the number of possible combinations of chemical mixes infinite. Some of the more commonly recorded symptoms of pesticide allergy are asthma attacks and breathing problems, skin irritation, personality change, mood swings, depression, nausea, malfunction of soft organs such as kidney, memory loss, swelling of soft tissue such as mouth and lips, and diarrhoea. People might mistakenly think that they are allergic to a particular food such as lettuce when in fact they are simply allergic to the pesticide applied to it during growing.

Long and slow poisoning effects

Long and slow (chronic) poisoning might be caused by daily ingestion of a very small dose of pesticides mainly through residues in food or from exposure at work. Symptoms of poisoning may not in some cases show for many years and it is very hard to attribute certain symptoms to one particular source. Doctors know very little about the possible long term effects of low doses of pesticides and therefore much illness is mis-diagnosed. Due to dissatisfaction with conventional methods of treatment some doctors have explored new avenues of treatment for the following:

Allergenic effects

Once an individual has shown an allergic reaction to a substance, the same reaction can recur, with different substances. For example, exposure to a pesticide may cause acute symptoms followed by the discovery of a marked sensitivity to a selection of different foods or other chemicals which produce inexplicable symptoms; the common factor is difficult to identify.

Environmental stress is likely to be a compounding factor in such a sensitized group of people. A combination of inappropriate behaviour and physical symptoms might show themselves as a result of the allergy, and everyday living may become difficult if not impossible to handle. This is no surprise if one stops to consider the enormous environmental changes man has had to cope with, particularly in the last 50 years. Our bodies cannot keep pace with the rapid rate of change expected from them. Men and women need to be able to choose an environment most suited to their own personalities. If they are forced to live and work in environmentally stressful conditions amidst noise, pollution, unpredictability, competition and aggression at a breakneck speed, their minds and bodies can suffer breakdown.

To lead as normal a life as possible free from allergic reactions you could, with some difficulty, embark on a restricted diet or try desensitization. A number of trained doctors offer tests and treatments for allergies (Mansfield and Monro, see page 188). Desensitization works by giving a vaccine containing small smounts of the offending substance to the patient and building up their resistance to it. This requires several repeat treatments and so immediate results cannot be expected.

Dental amalgam and mercury

Dental materials are placed permanently in the mouth, practically all of these materials corrode, yet the possible effects on health of these corrosion products are either insufficiently monitored or not monitored at all. The most commonly used material is mercury.

Mercury toxicity

The toxicity of mercury is well established. It is one of the most poisonous substances known to mankind. The University of Tennessee has a renowned toxicology centre where they grade poisons on the basis of the least amount necessary to kill a human being. Plutonium is the most deadly and is rated on their scale at 1900, mercury at 1600 and nickel at 600.

Dental amalgam fillings contain approximately 50 per cent mercury.

Historical background

Amalgam fillings were first introduced as a cheap replacement material for gold in the early part of the 19th century. In 1845 The American Society of Dental Surgeons passed a resolution 'pronouncing the use of all amalgam as malpractice' and further demanded that each member sign a pledge not to use amalgams, or be expelled from the Society. But commercial considerations prevailed, and amalgam fillings became the main restorative material for decayed teeth. The battle has continued in varying degrees of intensity until the present day, when new research material is beginning to alter entrenched positions.

The current position

For 150 years or so, it has been consistently maintained that mercury is locked into the amalgam filling and cannot escape and therefore could pose no health problem. Recent research however shows that mercury is released from these fillings, 24 hours a day, 7 days a week, and the volume may increase 15-fold when chewing, especially hot or acidic foods. Furthermore the amount released can be as much as 18 times the allowable daily limits established by some countries for mercury exposure from all sources in the environment.

Mercury deposits in the body

The primary organs for the accumulation of mercury are brain and central nervous system, kidneys, lungs, heart muscle, liver and red blood cells. Other storage areas are thyroid, pituitary and adrenal glands, spleen, testes, bone marrow, skeletal muscle and intestinal wall.

Studies on brain autopsy materials have shown that mercury deposited in the brain correlates directly with the surface area of amalgam fillings in the mouth and is independent of the sources found in food.

Mercury, dental amalgams and the immune system

Despite anything the science of medicine may have achieved, the immune system is our main defence against disease. Immune competence is dependent on total T-cells and the ratio of the variety of T-cells to one another. Reduction in total T-cells and unbalanced ratios can result in auto-immune disorders such as Systemic lupus erythematosus, multiple sclerosis, severe atopic eczema, inflammatory bowel disease and glomerulonephritis.

In May 1984, a preliminary paper by the Clinical Associate Professor, University of Southern California, discussed three cases, two involving amalgam and one involving nickel. In all three he demonstrated that the immune system was adversely affected – and substantially so – when the amalgam or nickel was present, and recovered on removal of the offending metals. By 1986 the Professor had 30 similar cases and will be publishing his findings when he has between 50-100.

Symptoms

Symptoms of this low level chronic exposure to mercury may vary enormously depending on the inherent reliance of the individual. Effects may be immediate. More often, however, the effects are insidious taking perhaps 5 years or more to show. Mercury may cause neurological, respiratory, cardiovascular and digestive disorders, interfere with collagen metabolism, and be implicated in food, chemical and inhalent allergies, and Candida and other fungal proliferations. Other effects may be local causing inflammation and gum diseases.

What percentage of the population is affected by amalgam fillings? Researchers estimates vary between 1 and 16%. Even 1 per cent would be 250,000 in Great Britain.

What the consumer can do

If you feel you are being affected by your amalgam fillings, then it is advisable to have them removed. You must remember that it is important to remove them in a certain order. This is determined by the electrical charge generated by each filling. For further advice on this matter consult a dental surgeon who has a grasp of the issue.

Diseases of the central nervous system

Pesticides in general work by interfering with the delicate mechanism of the central nervous system in pests.

The central nervous system consists of the brain and the spinal cord. A better way of explaining how the brain affects the whole of the body is to consider a car accident victim who suffers immediate brain damage which results in, possibly, the loss of use of legs, arms and other areas of the body. Some pesticides may be capable of very slowly damaging brain cells; the physical effects of this damage may not be seen for many years.

One of the diseases of the central nervous system is Parkinson's disease. James Parkinson first described its symptoms in 1817, but to date no cause has been proven. It affects 100,000 individuals in Britain alone.

The symptoms often become apparent in middle or old age with difficulties in controlling bodily movements. Head and limbs shake and there is difficulty in starting to move, but once on the move a walk can turn into a run. Normal activities such as eating, dressing and washing that require a moderate amount of muscular control become more difficult. After many years of slow degeneration the prospect could be of months or possibly years spent in a hospital bed completely rigid and possibly demented.

This reflects the almost complete destruction of an area of the brain that plays a key role in voluntary movement. The disease attacks a group of brain cells called *substantia nigra*. The substantia nigra sends nerve fibres to a structure called the *striatum* at the base of the forebrain.

The ends of these fibres produce a neurotransmitter *dopamine*

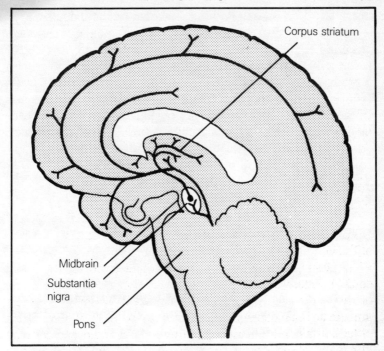

(neurotransmitters are the brain chemicals that carry information from one cell to another). In Parkinson's disease the almost total loss of brain cells that produce dopamine effectively cripple the striatum. This results in the physical symptoms previously described.

Research into the disease has now made it possible to devise a hypothesis about its origin. What is most certain is that the disease does not begin with the physical symptoms. It seems most likely that the affected areas of the brain degenerate very slowly over a number of years. This slow breakdown of brain cells could be happening throughout an apparently normal childhood or adolescence. The search is now on for an environmental factor(s) such as toxic chemicals, a virus or an imbalance of minerals as the trigger factor for the ongoing destruction of brain cells.

After years of very little progress in looking for a cause, an unexpected event led to the opening up of a completely new line of enquiry. A television documentary entitled *The Frozen Addict* described the step by step analysis of a medical one-off. It began in the San José jail in 1982. A 42-year-old drug addict prisoner,

George Carillo, awoke to find that he could neither talk or walk. He was apparently completely 'frozen' (immobile). He was transferred to Valley Medical Centre where, according to chief neurologist Dr J.W. Langston, doctors 'had never before seen such a case.'

The trail led to the underground drug world of California. Although George Carillo was the first of many, it soon became clear that all these 'frozen' victims had used a bad batch of a synthetic heroin – a so-called designer drug, which caused irreparable brain damage in all of its users. Something in this synthetic heroin had selectively destroyed a small patch of their brain cells, exactly the same area of cells that are killed in Parkinson's disease. In order to 'unfreeze' the drug victims, Dr Langston gave large doses of L-Dopa (the drug used to combat Parkinson's). It restored full mobility but all the victims will have to take this medicine every few hours for the rest of their lives.

To gain scientific value from this sad event the contaminant in the synthetic heroin was isolated. It was found to be 1-methyl-4-phenyl-1, 2, 3, 6, tetrahydropyridine or MPTP, a substance which destroys the same brain cells as those destroyed in Parkinson's disease.

Subsequent research by the late Dr André Barbeau linked the work on MPTP with a possible environmental cause for Parkinson's disease. Dr Barbeau was looking at the distribution of Parkinson's disease in a variety of areas in Canada. He found that the area of highest prevalence was the 'Garden of Quebec', an area of commercial vegetable farms. It is also an area that uses the largest amount of pesticides in Canada. The herbicide most widely used in the Garden of Quebec is Cyperquat which has a very similar chemical structure to that of the contaminant in the synthetic heroin, MPTP (1-methyl-4-phenyl-1, 2, 3, 6, tetrahydropyridine).

Dr Barbeau has also shown that patients with Parkinson's are three times more likely than others to suffer from liver problems which make them unable to break down toxic chemicals in their bodies and render them safe. These patients are therefore particularly susceptible to environmental insults.

A high incidence of Parkinson's disease is also found in areas near Canadian saw mills processing wood for paper manufacture. A connection between the chemicals used in wood processing and the disease could ultimately emerge. This brings together the case for an environmental cause. Dr Barbeau commented that: 'We should however stress that in these rural areas pesticides are not the only environmental contaminants. Soil, nature, air pollutants, animal faeces, contaminated water and many other factors must also be considered. All we have done to date is to identify one of the possible contaminants. Nobody has yet proven that pesticides are an actual cause for Parkinson's disease.'

Another interesting facet of Dr Barbeau's work is that he found Parkinson's disease to be less common in smokers than in non-smokers. A brief explanation to a very complicated subject could be that each person's liver handles toxic chemicals quite differently and every one has their own individual tolerance level.

Dr Barbeau's recent death has slowed down the very important research into environmental causes of the disease. It is vital for our long term good health that it is fully investigated by impartial researchers. A starting point could be looking into the childhood environment of sufferers.

Professor C.D. Marsden, a member of the Parkinson's Disease Society's medical advisory panel has asked for a large scale epidemiological survey in Britain to prove or disprove Dr Barbeau's work. The Commons Select Committee on Agriculture is gathering information, mainly from Dr Barbeau's work. The findings of the Committee will in due course be submitted to the appropriate Department of State, which will then decide if a bill is required. Those who feel that further research is vital should contact the Parkinson's Disease Society, 36 Portland Place, London W1N 3DG (Tel: 01-323 1174) who will direct you to the appropriate Government office.

Diseases of the central nervous system affecting behaviour

If one particular area of the brain is damaged then physical symptoms sometimes occur, e.g., Parkinsonism. Should damage occur in brain cell areas affecting behaviour very different symptoms are seen. Should chemicals such as pesticides or hydrocarbons, be absorbed into the brain, that can then interfere with the production of chemicals which enable nerve messages to travel from one area of the brain to another, then behavioural problems can be seen. These behavioural problems can be depression, lethargy, malaise, bouts of hyperactivity, attempted suicide, irrationality, loss of appetite, introversion, inability to handle even the simplest of tasks and general personality breakdown.

Doctors may tell patients suffering from any of these symptoms that they are due to causes such as a recent bereavement, marital problems, poor housing conditions, unemployment etc. They are given anti-depressants and sent away without the real cause being found.

Teratogenic effects and miscarriages

Teratogenic effects become apparent when the normal development of a foetus does not occur. This can happen at any time during a pregnancy and the baby is subsequently born deformed in some way.

Thalidomide was a drug given to women to relieve sickness in early pregnancy. The teratogenic effect of this drug was not fully realized until the required research had been carried out and a definite link established. In the meantime women were still taking this drug and sadly having deformed babies. Thalidomide affected the development of the foetus in the early stages of pregnancy when the extremitites are developing.

Thalidomide shows how a chemical can interfere with the normal development of a foetus during pregnancy. Isolating the cause and effect of thalidomide, now withdrawn, was fairly easy. Identifying any teratogenic effects of pesticides has been much more difficult. A pesticide shown to have possible teratogenic effects is 2,4,5-T.

2,4,5-T (2,4-5, trichlorophenoxy acetic acid) is a herbicide which kills by stimulating growth of the plant so that it eventually collapses and dies under its own weight. Recently it has become the focus of a major campaign by trade unions in Britain which want it banned. 2,4,5-T first came to the public's attention during the Vietnam War when the Americans sprayed millions of gallons of Agent Orange as a defoliant, the aim being to destroy cover for the Vietnamese. The main components of Agent Orange were 2,4,5-T and a related compound 2,4-D. Agent Orange also contained TCDD – Dioxin, which is one of the most potent carcinogens and teratogens known. According to Vietnamese scientists, examination of South Vietnamese refugees and North Vietnamese exposed to the herbicide by direct spraying or by eating contaminated food has shown a far greater incidence of various clinical abnormalities, including birth defects, miscarriages and sterility (Ref. Hay, 1982 – *The Chemical Scythe* – Plenum Press, London) than should have been expected.

There appears to be conflicting interpretation of the evidence about pesticides, particularly about 2,4,5-T. Until effects are recorded and correctly interpreted, any link between pesticides and birth defects will remain hidden.

If miscarriage and birth defects occurred in the animal world at the same rate as they do in humans the veterinary profession would start looking for environmental and dietary causes. In this country the actual number of miscarriages in humans is never fully recorded, nor are foetuses ever examined (or only possibly after you have experienced five or six miscarriages). Therefore, if environmental contaminants cause miscarriages we are simply failing to recognize the warning signs, largely because no one is collecting the data. Doctors say miscarriages are nature's way of disposing of imperfect foetuses – but they do not examine these foetuses to find out whether they are imperfect. There is a definite reluctance to carry out research into possible environmental causes for miscarriages.

It is not impossible for a member of the public to have an investigation carried out, however. Silicon Valley, California, changed from fruit and vegetable production to the manufacture of computers and silicon chips during the 1980s. Vast quantities of 1.1.1 Tichloroethane (also used as thinner for the correction fluid Tipp-Ex) are used for cleaning the silicon microchips. This chemical has to be stored underground in sealed tanks.

A mother living in the immediate vicinity of a major microchip producer, gave birth to a baby girl with severe congenital heart defects. She found out that virtually all the women in the area had suffered multiple miscarriages, stillbirths or birth defects in their children. This incidence had to be more than a quirk of nature. As the mothers checked each possibility they discovered that the water supply to the area was severely contaminated with 1.1.1-Trichloroethane. This chemical contamination was traced back to leaking storage tanks at the silicone chip factories. As a result of this discovery, one factory was forced to close and the others (at a cost of several millions dollars) replaced their storage tanks and now regularly monitor for contaminated water.

While carrying out research for this book we have found additional documented evidence positively linking pesticides with miscarriage. This example shows an association with the increase in spontaneous abortion with the use of 2,4,5-T in Oregon, USA. As a result, a temporary ban was imposed on the use of 2,4,5-T on forestry and rights of way. We feel that ultimately, more thorough research into this area should be carried out to reduce the number of miscarriages and help solve the congenital abnormality problem.

Kidney failure and liver damage

As this seldom becomes apparent at the time of exposure it is difficult to attribute kidney failure and liver damage to exposure from pesticides. From tests carried out on animals it is proven that Lindane (insecticide) and pentachlorophenol (PCP) (Fungicide) cause liver and kidney damage. Humans can be similarly affected, however, as documented in an article in *Roof* Shelter's housing magazine (May/June 1987).

A German family treated their home with a fungicide containing 6 per cent PCP. They suffered eye irritation, constant vomiting, exhaustion and liver damage. Friends visiting the house long after the fungicide application complained of similar symptoms. Three years later the mother gave birth to a daughter. She seemed always in a daze, could not stand upright and was prescribed physiotherapy by doctors. When she was one year old, the baby was found dead in her cot. She was covered in sweat and twisted by cramp. Though the death certificate simply read 'sudden infant death', a University doctor told the parents that her liver was enlarged and tests in Sweden found PCP dioxins in her internal organs. This was four years after the PCP had been applied in the home.

Cancer and mutagenic effects

Death from cancer is increasing. OPCS – 1978 *Trends in mortality 1951-75* – Series D.H.1 No.3 (Government Paper) reads: 'A major cause of this increase is due to massive increases in lung cancer since the last war, but there have also been relative increases in deaths from leukaemia, bladder and pancreatic cancers, and in women breast cancers, cancer of the ovaries and pancreas. Since 1971 an increase has been found in the rate of intestinal cancer among men.'

In spite of the difficulty of conducting epidemiological studies on the toxicology of pesticides a number of studies have sought to link occupational exposure of, for example, farmers with mortality data for the cause of death. These have appeared to demonstrate links between occupational exposure and leukaemia, lymphomas, prostate cancer, melanoma, multiple myeloma and stomach cancer (e.g., Burmeister et al, 1983, Blair, 1982). On the basis of a similar study it has been suggested that 0.5 per cent of cancer in America may be caused by pesticide exposure (Pimental and Perkins, 1980).

Certain types of pesticides are potentially more carcinogenic than others. Pesticides that break down easily (e.g., organophosphates) are unlikely to have any lasting effect. On the other hand, those that are persistent will have the ability to cause ill health because they are more often found as food residues.

In the United States, a clause in the food legislation forbids the inclusion in any food of any chemical identified as a possible human carcinogen. This supports the idea that there is *no safe level* for a carcinogen. In the USA all toxicology testing is carried out by independent scientists, whereas in Britain testing is massively dominated by industry.

It has been clearly established that DDT causes leukaemia and lung and liver cancer in successive generations of mice. Some experts will tell you that you cannot correlate cause and effect of chemicals between different species. But we know from the 1985 MAFF report on pesticide residues that DDT, although officially banned in the UK, is present as a residue in our food, body fat and human milk. You can draw your own conclusions.

Mutagenicity

Mutagens are chemicals which damage the genetic material of the body's cells. If this occurs in reproductive cells the harmful change(s) may be passed on to future generations.

There is much evidence implicating the mutagenicity of a wide number of pesticides permitted for use on foods. At least 61 commonly used pesticides, permitted for use on foods have been implicated as mutagens or suspected mutagens in animals. Some common carbamates, such as aldicarb, carbaryl and carbofuran, may not be directly mutagenic. However, these insecticides can be converted to nitrosamines fairly readily in the human stomach, due to their containing a secondary amino group in their chemical structure (see page 77 for details on nitrosamines).

There are grounds for caution in the use of all pesticides on foods once they have been implicated as a mutagen.

At risk groups

The following groups of people are at risk from the toxic effects of chemicals/pesticides for a variety of reasons. This list is in no way comprehensive and only includes those who immediately come to mind.

● **Farm workers**
Can be exposed to a cocktail of pesticides, by working in an agro-chemically based farming system. Those working on organic farms will obviously be at less risk, another sound reason for advocating the organic way of farming. Farm workers come into contact with toxic chemicals in the following ways: by preparing solutions from dry powders, during actual application to the ground, by accident, spillage, disposing of empty containers, skin contact and inhalation of spray vapours. The importance of following manufacturers' instructions should not be underestimated. Sadly very few checks are ever made. The temptation during warm weather not to wear protective clothing and masks must be great. Even though safety precautions are time-consuming and a nuisance, manufacturers should emphasize to the user the importance of following the instructions on every occasion.

● **Workers in the manufacturing processes of pesticides**
Trade unions have a significant role to play in ensuring that workers are working in a safe environment. It is often through their taking up of personal issues that occupational hazards are identified and precautionary measures taken. Once safety measures have been decided upon, health and safety officers must ensure that safety precautions are adhered to on a daily basis. An employee should be taken to task over sloppy work practices. In the event of an

industrial accident employees should be taught the correct emergency procedures.

● People spending leisure time in the countryside

Millions of people are at risk especially at weekends and holiday times from contamination in the countryside: ramblers; walkers; campers; golfers; cyclists; riders and picnickers. They can be inadvertently sprayed by aerial and tractor spraying; children may eat treated crops such as a head of corn; swimming or paddling in contaminated rivers and streams; walking through a field of treated crops and brushing against them. The following is taken from the *Rambler*, the official magazine of the Rambling Association (April 1987):

Pesticide Path Danger: Agriculture Minister Michael Jopling may tell farmers to see that crops sprayed with certain pesticides are kept well back from public rights of way to ensure that members of the public do not come into contact with chemicals.

Mr Jopling added that his department 'will be giving detailed consideration during 1987 to the terms on which the conditions of approval (for pesticides) are given statutory effect next year. Where a pesticide remains an irritant on the crop after spraying,' he continued, 'it may be necessary to require that farmers keep the crop sufficiently far from public footpaths to avoid skin contact by walkers.'

This new promise was made to RA vice-president Lord Melchett, who had earlier called for an urgent review of the potential health hazards to country walkers of 27 pesticides and other chemicals approved for use by farmers and growers. 'Walkers are threatened by a silent and hidden menace in the countryside,' Lord Melchett said.

According to the most recent information, 13 of the chemicals on Lord Melchett's 'danger list' are officially classified as poisonous substances; 14 are referred to as dangerous or harmful to animals; and 19 are approved for aerial spraying.

Lord Melchett urged the minister to ban the spraying on or near public paths of all pesticides except those that Mr Jopling could *guarantee* would do no harm to walkers and their children.

Some of the most hazardous chemicals are used in the cultivation of fruit or hops. For example, Methumyl is an insecticide used in hop cultivation. It is a registered poisonous substance and hop growers are recommended to ensure that no 'unprotected persons' enter the field for at least one day after spraying.

Those living near arable farm land can be exposed to a number of chemicals. The hazards of living in the countryside are grossly underestimated. Living in the countryside is portrayed as 'idyllic', – perhaps it was 100 years ago, but not now!

● Pest infestation controllers
The people who spray houses for woodworm, cockroaches, rodents etc. are potentially at greatest risk from pesticide poisoning as they are in daily contact with a variety of different chemicals in an enclosed situation. One of the biggest dangers associated with the toxicity of pesticides is dealing with them in their wet state. It is vital for the health of such workers that *all* the safety precautions available are strictly followed.

● People living or working in pesticide-treated buildings
The law stating that buildings should be vacated until smells disperse is no guarantee that the building is then safe to work or live in. As 30-year guarantees are given for the prevention of re-infestation this is an indication of how long pesticides can remain active – and cause ill health and possibly death for occupants or workers in the building.

● The health conscious
We are now actively encouraged to eat more fresh fruit and vegetables but this can actually increase intake of any pesticide residues in the food. This should not, however, deter you from eating fresh fruit and vegetables because of their obvious nutritional value. The answer is to eat your fruit and vegetables washed and peeled or ideally, to eat residue-reduced foods.

● Pregnant and breast-feeding women and their babies
Evidence for these being at risk lies in the fact that pesticide residues have been found in human body fat and human milk. The possibility always exists for pesticide residues to pass through the placenta to the developing baby, and for breast-fed babies to receive residues via the mother's milk. It should not be assumed that modified cow's milk is any better. It is not. The answer is to have residue-reduced foods and milk.

● The general public
No matter what you are told there are *no safe* levels for a poison. All the poisons used on our foodstuffs will have some effect. Such

effects are not, unfortunately, being recognized or monitored adequately. A tragic example of how vulnerable we are as members of the general public was shown by the mysterious symptoms that developed in parts of Spain in May 1981. Unscrupulous street traders had sold unlabelled bottles of oil of unknown origin as pure olive oil mostly to the poorer sectors of the community. Initially people were pleased to buy the cheap oil as the Spanish use as much as five litres of oil a week per family. Gradually, however, large numbers of people became ill. The symptoms of the sufferers were diverse and not easily explained by known methods of pathology. In May 1981 acute cases were recorded of fever, rashes, myalgia and respiratory disorders. Most of the deaths were due to a pneumonopathy. Cases still continued to arrive at hospitals well into June and July 1981 but with different symptoms. These were intense muscular pain, numbness of arms and legs and thrombo-embolism sometimes set in. By August and September patients were again experiencing a change in symptoms. There was swelling under the skin with other complications including ulceration and lesions, difficulty in swallowing, weakness in muscles, emaciation, actual growing smaller and frailer and simply wasting away. After investigations, the sickness was traced back to the cheap oil and the selling of the oil was stopped. Although there has never been any conclusive analysis of the oil there are two plausible explanations:

Firstly, the oil used could have been contaminated by excessive pesticide use on the crop. An explanation for this is that the oil grown for industrial use only is often heavily pesticided. Secondly, the oil was meant for industrial use only, so a toxic chemical might have been added to it to deter people from using it for culinary use. Other theories are still being considered. The net result is that 100 people have lost their lives and over 13,000 people have been affected in one way or another.

To safeguard your and your family's health, a move towards eating residue-reduced foods and foods of known origin is advisable. The best way to be 100 per cent confident of what you are eating is to grow your own and *not* to use agro-chemicals that are heavily advertised as the only answer to every gardener's problem but to cultivate your produce organically, without harmful chemical fertilizers or sprays.

Practical pointers

● Unions look after workers in various ways, but one of the most vital areas is health and safety at work. It is essential for the worker to follow *good* working practices, but also to alert unions to potential working hazards. It is then up to the unions to negotiate with the management to revise and improve working conditions. It should also be the responsibility of the employers to monitor staff and give regular health check-ups. If you are working in the pesticide or other potentially hazardous industry and not receiving frequent medical check-ups, this matter should be brought to the union's attention. This would go some way towards preventing chronic illness in later life due to exposure of pesticides and other contaminants.

● There should be a move towards keeping spraying away from the general public and restricting the use of pesticides near walkways and paths. Aerial spraying should be restricted to night time only and a structured plan to ban aerial spraying altogether should be formulated. If you feel strongly about this write to the Ramblers' Association, 1/5 Wandsworth Road, London SW8 2XX and to Friends of the Earth, 24 Underwood Street, London N1 (Tel: 01-490-1555). FoE operates Spray watch, a network of local pesticide incident recorders, and would like to know date, place and name of offending farmers. Copies of letters should also be sent to the farmer, the National Farmers' Union and your local MP.

● The leading authority on the treatment of patients exposed to contaminants is Dr Jean Monro. It is possible to be treated by her and other doctors in this field at The Lister Hospital, Allergy and Environmental Medicine Dept, Chelsea Bridge Road, London SW1W 8RH (Tel: 01-730 3417); and the Breakspear Hospital, Abbots Langley, Hertfordshire WD4 9HT (Tel: 09277 61333).
    This is a possible course of action if you feel frustrated with the treatment provided by your local GP. Sadly this expertise is not available on the NHS, so be prepared to pay for the treatment.

● As there is no labelling for pesticide/contaminant content of food, we do not really know what we are eating. The only practical alternative is to eat organically grown foods and drink filtered water. If you do not live near Safeways or other producers of organic food then keep asking your local supermarket to provide it. The more

people do this the more likely the supermarkets will be to stock
organic foods and see it as a profitable venture.

● Ensure better practice in the use of pesticides. One idea, from
consultant David Stephens, would be to require pesticides to contain
a fluorescent chemical which would enable residues in food to be
readily detected by an inexpensive ultra-violet light. An ultra violet
light could also be used by farmers before harvesting a crop to ensure
that residues had been washed off.

● If you are unhappy with the present situation you can contact,
among others, your local MP, your local water authority, the local
supermarket and the Ministry of Agriculture, Food and Fisheries.
Also the Department of Health and Social Security, Hannibal
House, Elephant and Castle, London SE1 6TE; the National Union
of Farmers, Agriculture House, Knightsbridge, London SW1X 7NJ
(Tel: 01-235 5077); Friends of the Earth (see above); the British
Medical Association, Tavistock Square, London WC1H 9JP.
   When writing to the Association you could state that generally
doctors know very little about the diagnosis and treatment of acute
and long term pesticide poisoning and that their training should
include this.

CHAPTER 2

Facts and figures
– other residues

Hormones

As members of the animal kingdom we all produce enough hormones for our body's essential development. Natural hormones are secreted by various glands and travel in the bloodstream to different parts of the body. They cause biological changes such as growth, muscle development and sexual maturity. These changes can be artificially boosted. For example, thyroxine is given to dairy cows to promote milk yields and to obtain more wool from sheep. Progesterones are given to control the oestrus cycle in sheep, pigs and cattle – in other words they are put on the 'pill'.

Hormones are also given to regulate the egg-laying cycle of poultry. Indeed, poultry seemed a splendid target for hormones. Intensive methods of rearing poultry led to the development of the capon – bigger than an ordinary chicken but small enough for a family meal. Capons are male birds whose testes are left intact but to speed up weight gain a pellet of synthetic female hormone hexoestrol was inserted under the skin in their necks. This process went on for some 20 years until concern over the safety of the hormones led to an official ban in 1982.

There have been numerous cases of hormone abuse. One example was the premature sexual maturing in young children in Milan who ate veal which had been treated with one of the female sex hormones from the Stilbene group. The Italian Government subsequently banned the drug.

Stilbenes

Stilbenes are a group of hormones which have been implicated in a number of different health problems. The most devastating occurred in America when doctors gave Di-ethylstilbestrol (DES) to women who had had a history of miscarriage. They successfully carried their babies to term but the girls later developed vaginal cancer and the boys developed cancer of the testes, usually at the onset of puberty. Stilbenes, nevertheless, are among the farmer's favourites. They cause rapid weight gain and can be easily injected into an animal, undetectable by inspection. The only way they can be identified is by an analysis of the animal under laboratory conditions.

In February 1986 the EEC, in response to consumer pressure throughout Europe decided to prohibit the use of growth-promoting hormones in livestock. Michael Jopling, Minister of Agriculture at that time, initially opposed the ban, which came into effect in January 1988. Although it is thought that this ban was due to consumer pressure it may have been politically motivated. The EEC wanted an acceptable way of reducing the food mountains. Banning a product that actively encourages weight gain in animals would help reduce the surpluses and allow the consumer to believe that he had actually influenced the EEC in this matter.

Anabolic steroids

These are added to animal feeds and are similar in their action to hormones. In fact, both possess the useful characteristic, as far as the farmer is concerned, of encouraging the growth of muscle tissue at the expense of fatty tissue. What happens is that the steroids promote lean rather than fatty meat. These too were banned by the EEC as from February 1988.

Whenever a ban is put on a substance, and when revenue might be lost, there is always the danger that the letter of the law might not be kept. Farmers could be tempted to stockpile hormones whilst they are still legally available. The shelf life of some of these hormones is up to five years. Once banned, there is always a 'black market' not just in Britain but in Europe as a whole. The worrying aspect of this is that because these drugs have been 'officially' banned the inspectorate will no longer be monitoring their use, and meat will not therefore be tested for excessive contamination. We must rely on the moral fibre of our farmers to consider the well-being of the consumer.

One substance that has received attention from the press is bovine somatotrophin (BST) (see the food chain connection, page 96). This substance, although it produces the same effect as a growth-promoting hormone, has not been banned to date, as it is cleverly described as a natural protein or milk yield improver. This description enables BST to pass through legislation easily. This type of loophole in the law should cause concern.

Other substances are used to promote growth in animals. The best known is copper. This is almost exclusively used as a feed additive for growing pigs. It can increase food conversion to body weight by nine per cent. It is only given to animals intended for slaughter, as surplus copper is stored in the liver and would therefore ultimately poison adult beasts that should provide the following year's offspring. The consumer may ask what happens to those contaminated pigs' livers? Do they reach the supermarkets?

It should also be noted that the recommended doses of copper apparently increase the animal's resistance to antibiotics in its gut. Animals receiving this copper supplement obviously produce manure that is rich in copper, making it unsuitable for use on the land. Sheep have been known to die after eating grass treated with copper-contaminated pig droppings.

Antibiotics

Antibiotics are used for medical purposes for both humans and animals. They are derived from moulds and other micro-organisms which have the ability to 'kill off' both harmful and therapeutic bacteria. It was found that animals which had been continually taking antibiotics gained weight. Antibiotics particularly increased the growth rate in young animals. What probably occurs is that the antibiotics kill any bacteria that might otherwise produce mild infections which farmers would fail to recognize. These mild infections slow down the rate at which an animal can gain weight, and so it will take longer to reach prime condition, costing the farmer more. Alternatively they could destroy any parasitic organism in the digestive system that would be competing for the animal's food.

Diseases such as pneumonia and dysentery that were so often fatal in the past can be cured by antibiotics. However, by 1953 farmers were able to add xylosin, penicillin and tetracycline to animal feed and they were routinely added to the diet of chickens and calves, particularly those intended for the veal market. It soon became apparent however, that some bacteria were becoming resistant to antibiotics. In the 1960s Britain was hit by a succession of salmonella outbreaks, mostly affecting young animals. During the course of treating the animals vets noticed that the bacteria were becoming increasingly resistant to antibiotics. As a result of this, thousands of animals died. What worried the authorities was that resistance could be carried over from one bacterial species to another. This is known technically as 'transferred drug resistance'. A later survey showed that more than 70 per cent of all strains of staphylococci in hospital patients are now resistant to penicillin. In 1968 the Swan Committee, chaired by Professor M.M. Swan, concluded that if antibiotics continued to be used for animal purposes, human beings would be at risk because there would be nothing left with which to treat them. The Committee made practical recommendations to prevent a science fiction state of becoming completely powerless to treat a common disease.

Antibiotics can be divided into two types. Firstly, those that are true medicines, in that they are used for humans as well as animals. To prevent misuse these types of antibiotics are obtainable only on a vet's prescription. Feed antibiotics, e.g., zinc bacitracin would only include antibiotics discarded for use in human medicine. Farmers could buy these without a prescription and the daily dose would be within levels that would prevent bacteria from developing resistance to them.

As we have already mentioned, as soon as the law introduces controls, manipulation and exploitation of any existing loopholes follows. The situation the Swan committee failed to recognize and prevent was that if a farmer could convince himself and his vet that his animals had been exposed to a disease and might become sick as a result, he could persuade the vet to write out a blanket prescription for the restricted medical antibiotics – just in case, of course!

The role of the vet

If a refusal to a client is appropriate a vet should stick to his guns, even at the risk of losing the custom. Hopefully, a farmer would respect the vet's decision and be willingly guided as to the most appropriate course of action to take in treating his animals. However, it is likely that some vets succumb to the pressures put on them. The result is that prescription-only antibiotics are finding their way into animals on a regular basis. Supporting this is the fact that microbiologists are still finding strains of resistant bacteria in our environment which could only realistically be coming from animal sources. As a protection for the consumer, pressure should be put upon the Government to reappoint the Swan Committee to tighten up the loopholes of the original Swan Report and to appoint qualified inspectors to monitor the use of antibiotics and other residues on farms and bring prosecution against those not complying.

Vets generally take up their profession because of a caring attitude towards animals. They should also take up the role of ambassadors to promote the humane treatment of animals, both domestic and farm. Taking away the welfare of animals from the hands of 'fringe' groups and into the hands of professionals would immediately upgrade the importance of animal welfare. Farmers need the guidance of a professional body to suggest practical and reasonable improvements in animal husbandry. Because of the extreme behaviour of certain groups, farmers have become reluctant to accept any criticism of their farming practices. This stalemate situation could be overcome by vets taking a more active interest in good husbandry techniques. Perhaps this should be included in the training of vets, enabling them to offer an all-round service to farmers. Finally, farmers should attend courses arranged not by the chemical giants but by the Consumers' Association which would inform them of what the consumers really want to buy.

Probiotics

As their name implies, probiotics are the opposite of antibiotics. They do not wipe out bacteria as a means of controlling disease-producing bacteria, as do antibiotics, but encourage the healthy bacteria that normally live in the intestines to grow more abundantly.

They could be used as another method of promoting good health.

The initial work on probiotics was carried out at Reading, based on the apparent healthgiving properties of yogurt. There are two main bacteria in yogurt – lactose bacillus bulgaricus and lactobacillus thermophillus. It has been held that, if taken regularly, these bacteria can keep the digestive system in good order, thereby preventing any takeover of harmful bacteria which might then cause illness. Sadly it has been found that claims commonly made for ordinary yogurt are spurious. The bacteria in ordinary yogurt do not survive long enough in the gut to reproduce and colonize it, so any health-giving properties are short-lived. However, other bacteria present in our stomachs have been cultured and suitable strains have been developed that encourage good health. So therefore, by eating probiotic yogurt we would have every chance to colonize our gut with healthy bacteria that could provide long-term beneficial effects.

These findings could have an enormous influence on animal husbandry. From February 1988 growth hormones were banned; this could be extended to all chemical growth promoters being withdrawn. If tests show that probiotics promote weight gain in animals without causing resistant strains as with antibiotics, this could open the gates for a completely new industry based on the therapeutic effects of some natural bacteria. Consumers must judge for themselves as to whether they feel happy about buying meat that has been artificially forced.

At risk groups

● Babies and young children

Those most vulnerable to the adverse effects of hormones that are fed to animals are babies and young children. This is because they are so small, and in the very early stages of growing any invasion of hormones will upset their development. For example, one of the Stilbene hormones, DES causes the acceleration of bone development and a child exposed to unknown quantities will have premature ageing of the bones even before they are fully developed. Although baby products are examined and have tests carried out on them, there seems to be no figures available for the average hormone content of modified baby milks or baby foods, nor is there any literature available to estimate acceptable maximum levels of hormones in babies and young children. This is most unsatisfactory.

● Pregnant and breast-feeding mothers

These are particularly vulnerable. A number of health problems can arise during a pregnancy, so it is important that pregnant women eat as healthily as possible. Many hormonal changes are going on in a pregnant woman's body and additional hormones from food could adversely affect this delicate balance. Nature is very careful in her use of hormones and any additional exposure through food could cause unnecessary risks.

Whilst breast-feeding, different hormonal releases take place. The invasion of hormones from food could affect the mother as well as the baby, whose normal development could be interfered with, causing irreversible damage. As babies' delicate organs are not fully operational, even minute quantities of hormones can cause problems. Although in February 1988 the use of growth hormones was banned there is a danger that some farmers more interested in profit margins than consumer health will continue to use them.

● The general public

Ordinary consumers are a low level risk group generally, but some individuals are particularly sensitive to hormonal changes. As there has never been any work carried out on the general public with regard to hormone levels (and following the recent ban there probably never will be), it is difficult to come to any definite conclusions on their influence. However, those who consume large quantities of animal produce, particularly organ meat such as liver and kidney which absorbs and retains most of the hormones, will be receiving significantly more hormone residues than the average person. As we are being encouraged to eat less meat because of its fat content, it is hoped that the situation will improve, helped along by organically produced meat becoming more readily available in the supermarkets.

Practical pointers

● The consumer will soon have the opportunity of buying meat produced to Soil Association standards – truly organic – or to conservative grade where only a limited selection of 'additives' are used. This will have far-reaching effects and will significantly reduce the residues in people's diets. Residue-reduced meat is available through a selection of regional butchers (see page 189) but some selected supermarkets will be offering a range of organic meat in the relatively near future. When shoppers recognize the true value of these products the organic industry will consequently develop to provide a wider variety of products and become far more competitive.

● Complaining constructively about non-organic products that are on the market at present is often thought to be wasted effort. However, Safeways, for example, keep all correspondence and do actually make moves on consumer demand. If you are not happy about the foods you buy in your supermarkets write to them explaining exactly what you are willing to buy, ask for fuller information as to where their meat comes from, ask about the quality of the land the animals were reared upon, what kind of living conditions they were subjected to and the results of analysis of the meat. If you, the customer, start asking for this level of information, according to the type of response received, you can decide whether or not you are happy with their standards.

Milk can also carry hormone residues. You might therefore write to the Milk Marketing Board to ask for details of hormone levels in milk. There are also alternatives to regular milk such as organic cow's milk and goat's milk and organic soya milk. The milkman could perhaps be persuaded to start delivering organic milk to your doorstep.

Many of the suggestions outlined in the *Practical pointers* sections throughout this book could be implemented most successfully by the National Farmers' Union. They have the knowledge and ability to lead farmers and growers along new paths of thought and development and could also pass comments to the farmers from the consumers. Many of the agricultural colleges throughout Britain could teach these new marketing skills to young farmers because they are probably the ones most able to bring about innovative change. The NFU could then design and implement refresher courses nationwide for farmers to attend, on many aspects of farming, from the safe handling of pesticides to organics, the new growth industry.

The milk quota situation which led to land being taken out of use because of surpluses need never have arisen. If there had been continual analysis of the situation, blunders of this magnitude would have been avoided.

● The Minister for Agriculture could eliminate the string of 'bad experiences' the consumer has to suffer at present, by introducing a team of impartial advisers whose job it would be to monitor all animals on farms and visit farms regularly, evaluating the methods of farming that were being carried out. These advisers should also have the power to close down farms where practices could be said to be dangerous to health. Doctors and health advisers should also help ensure that suitable foods are grown to an acceptable standard. If the food industry was organized on a foundation of sound nutrition and a residue-reduced policy, the potential for better health would be immense. We are only just beginning to realize the connection between contaminated food and ill health. All new findings must be used to influence government policy to prevent risk to consumers.

Aluminium

Aluminium is a silvery white ductile metallic element and the most abundant metal found in the earth's crust. It is present in combination with other elements as, for example, in bauxite. Because of its qualities of being hard, light, and corrosion-resistant, it has found its way into everyday use. Many forms of aluminium have been devised by scientists and are now used routinely as additives or adjuncts in many areas. Approximately half the aluminium in the diet comes from cereals and other vegetable matter but these naturally occuring forms are not absorbed. Most soluble forms that *are* absorbed are present because of the deliberate addition of aluminium salts to food and medicines; the incidental introduction of aluminium during cooking with aluminium utensils; and residual aluminium from the use of aluminium salts in the treatment of many water supplies.

Aluminium salts are used widely in the food industry as emulsifying, anti-caking, bleaching and raising agents. Baking powders may contain as much as five per cent aluminium by weight and processed cheese may contain up to 0.5 per cent by weight.

Aluminium salts are widely used in preserving or pickling processes, and in powdered foods such as instant coffee, dried milk, artificial 'creamers' and table salt. Codes indicating the presence of aluminium or aluminium salts include E173, E541, E554, E556. Tea leaves contain high levels of aluminium and brewed tea contains amounts as high as those added in the treatment of drinking water. You will not see it labelled on tea packets, however.

Aluminium salts are used frequently as buffering compounds in drugs such as aspirin. The largest amounts occur in some antacids where the recommended daily dose may be equivalent to 1-2 grammes of elemental aluminium. Aluminium hydroxide and aluminium carbonate appear to be more readily absorbed from the gut than aluminium phosphate. Antacids, containing magnesium trisilicate are free from aluminium, are available and you should ask your doctor to prescribe this type and not the aluminium-rich variety.

Aluminium occurs naturally in many upland sources of water and in a few ground waters used for drinking water supplies. The aluminium concentrations in some sources may be increased as a consequence of acid rain. Much of the aluminium is complexed by naturally occurring organic substances or may be in colloidal form and is not readily absorbed from the gut. However, since the 1920s aluminium salts have been used to treat many water supplies, principally to remove brown, peaty discoloration caused by some organic substances. An EEC directive which came into effect in July 1985 imposes a maximum concentration of 200µg/l (200 parts per 1,000 million) for aluminium in drinking water supplies. In some cases where aluminium salts are used in water treatment the residual concentrations exceed this limit and the water authorities/companies concerned have programmes of improvement which will be completed mainly by 1990 to ensure that the directive is met. The Government has granted permission for this level to be exceeded in a few cases where natural aluminium concentrations are above the limit.

If you are concerned about the aluminium levels in your area write to your local water authority for details. Should you not be satisfied with their reply, then make your dissatisfaction clearly known and felt.

Aluminium cookware can be found in every hardware shop and because it is usually fairly cheap, most people possess at least one aluminium saucepan. Aluminium pressure cookers, teapots, kettles, frying pans, cake tins, baking trays and large utensils are also readily used in hospitals and canteens.

Aluminium is rapidly oxidized in air and the surface layer of oxide which forms is not dissolved under mild acidic or alkaline conditions. However, under stronger acid conditions such as cooking with tomatoes or marmalade making, the surface layer is dissolved and relatively large amounts of aluminium are released. The most acidic foods such as rhubarb, spinach, cabbage etc., or sauces containing vinegar, dissolve aluminium utensils very effectively, as evidenced by the interior surface of the pan after cooking. Also, recent evidence suggests that the presence of only 1 part per million of fluoride (the permitted level of fluoridation) in water used to cook acidic foods may greatly increase the liberation of aluminium. It has been claimed that the final levels reached with this combination may be 2,500-3,000 times the maximum permitted levels for addition to drinking water. However, there is some evidence that fluoride may also inhibit the absorption of aluminium from the gastro-intestinal tract and could be beneficial in this respect. Studies are in progress to determine whether fluoridation causes a decrease in the availability of aluminium. It will take a number of years to establish the findings on this matter, but perhaps fluoridization should stop until the matter is adequately investigated even if dentists are totally opposed to it. It also puts the question of fluoride applications on childrens' teeth under the spotlight.

Dialysis dementia

The question most people will want to know is 'Does aluminium have any health risks attached to it?' Dr Phillip Day from Manchester University became involved with a group of doctors anxious about some renal patients on dialysis. They were experiencing speech disorders, poor memory, lack of concentration and personality changes which led to loss of muscle co-ordination, total dementia, and in some cases death. The doctors were puzzled at this and finally came to the conclusion that the water used in the dialysis of these patients was somehow implicated. As a dialysis patient is exposed to 180 litres of water every session and may have up to four sessions a week it seemed a reasonable assumption. These symptoms occurred in patients who had been on dialysis for several years and was first noted in the mid 1970s.

Dr Day was asked to investigate, and discovered that aluminium levels were related to the dementia suffered by the renal patients. He also found that there were regional variations around Britain with high levels of aluminium in the water in Scotland, the North of England, and low levels in London and the South East. Where the aluminium was found in the greatest quantity he also found the highest incidence of dialysis dementia. Even within the small area of Greater Manchester he noted variations in aluminium levels in the water. These depended on the source. If it came from peaty, upland areas it had a brown tinge and so was treated with aluminium to remove the discoloration.

To make the connection between aluminium and dialysis dementia clear, we should explain that the kidneys in young, normal, healthy people can remove aluminium from the blood and so no problems arise. However, in patients with kidney disease, aluminium levels can rise in the blood and become deposited in the brain and bones causing dementia and bone disorders.

Dr Day presented his findings to the Department of Health and Social Security in order to get dialysis grade water for renal patients. This is water with the lowest possible level of aluminium (present EEC tap water level is 200 mgs per 1 litre, but Dr Day wanted to see dialysis patients receiving water containing less than 20 mgs per 1 litre). His findings were initially rejected on the basis that it would be too expensive to install the necessary equipment to treat ordinary tap water in all dialysis units, even though a number of people were dying as a result of the aluminium in the water. Eventually, after much pressure was applied, the DHSS agreed to pay for dialysis grade water to be produced for all renal units in Britain. Since 1980 no cases of dialysis dementia have been recorded in Manchester, where previously five to ten deaths were recorded per year.

Alzheimer's disease

The recent findings of Professor J.A. Edwardson working at the Medical Research Council Unit at Newcastle General Hospital point to aluminium as a possible contributory factor in the development of Alzheimer's disease.

Alzheimer's disease is the most common form of senile dementia, a disease marked by severe progressive memory loss and breakdown of personality. It occurs much more rarely in people of middle age but in all cases it is accompanied by degenerative changes in the brain. There is a marked loss of brain cells, particularly in regions concerned with the control of memory, orientation and personality. Two characteristic lesions appear in the brain in large numbers. One of these is the 'senile plaque', a minute area of brain damage (about 0.05-0.1mm in diameter) in which disordered nerve processes and nerve-endings surround a microscopic extracellular deposit of material, the so-called 'plaque core'. The other typical lesion is the 'neurofibrillary tangle' an abnormal deposit of protein fibrils which occurs within damaged nerve cells. Both plaques and tangles may occur in huge numbers in the brains of patients with Alzheimer's disease.

To give some idea of the size of the problem it is estimated that as many as 500,000 elderly people in the UK suffer from a moderate or severe dementia and research shows that almost two thirds of these have the characteristic changes of Alzheimer's disease. As the number and proportion of elderly in the population increases, Alzheimer's disease has become one of the largest problems facing the health and social services. It appears that due to lack of funding the NHS will not be able to offer any preventive measures, or little support for sufferers immediately.

The cause of Alzheimer's disease has not yet been isolated, but the disease sometimes runs in families in a way which strongly indicates a genetic contribution. Most sufferers from Down's syndrome (or 'mongolism' as it was formerly known) develop the characteristic lesions associated with Alzheimer's disease by the age of 40. Down's syndrome is caused by the presence of an extra copy of chromosome 21 and it has been shown recently that the gene for a protein associated with some pathological changes in Alzheimer's disease is located on chromosome 21. Fragments of this protein are one component of the senile plaque core and they also occur in abnormal deposits around the blood vessels of the brain in Alzheimer's disease. This protein may also give rise to the neurofibrillary tangles. Evidence in *Science*, (13 March 1987) suggests that some sufferers from Alzheimer's disease have a short duplicated section of chromosome 21 which may be responsible for the disorder. However, the enormous range in the time of onset and the severity of neurodegenerative changes suggest that environmental influences also play an important role. There is evidence pointing to a variety of factors including slow virus infections, environmental toxins, auto-immune disease and disordered mineral metabolism. On this list, aluminium has frequently reappeared as a possible cause.

A growing body of evidence, albeit circumstantial, links aluminium with Alzheimer's disease.

● Aluminium is one of the very few substances known to cause 'tangles' in the brains of susceptible species. Although the tangles produced in experimental animals with aluminium are not identical to those occuring in man, they are very similar.

● It has been shown that in Alzheimer's disease, the cellular content of aluminium is higher in tangle-bearing nerve cells than in adjacent, undamaged nerve cells.

● There is a focal deposit of aluminium combined with silicon (aluminosilicate) at the heart of the senile plaque core, which is surrounded by damaged nerve-processes.

● Aluminium is the cause of 'dialysis dementia', a condition in which patients undergoing dialysis for kidney disease develop severe memory loss and many other neuropathological changes. These changes differ from those in Alzheimer's disease but the brain areas involved are similar and increased numbers of nerve cells with neurofibrillary tangles are seen in this condition.

● Aluminium levels are also raised in the tangle-bearing neurones present in a rare disease of the Western Pacific – the so-called 'Parkinsonian dementia complex' of Guam. This disorder occurs among isolated groups of natives and has been linked (among other possible causes) to a chronic environmental deficiency of calcium and magnesium and high exposure to aluminium in the local water.

● Treatment of experimental animals with injections of aluminium has been shown to cause severe memory loss. It appears that aluminium is selectively accumulated by those brain regions which are most affected in Alzheimer's disease e.g., the hippocampus, important for memory function.

● There is some controversial epidemiological evidence suggesting higher prevalence rates for dementia in areas with high environmental levels of aluminium.

Should we be looking at all forms of aluminium? Aluminium from many sources is present in dust but there is no evidence that inhalation is normally a significant route of exposure. However, some workers are subject to exposure from dust containing very high levels of aluminium or aluminium compounds. These include workers in primary production plants and those using aluminium powder for cold-casting, finger-printing etc. Unfortunately there does not appear to be a reliable long term follow-up study of those exposed to aluminium in this way but this is being planned at the present moment. A large-scale study to investigate whether exposure to aluminium powder causes increased blood levels is in progress and the findings will be presented in due course.

Aluminium is also found as a major component of some anti-perspirant deodorant sticks or sprays. This does not seem, however, to be a problem as the skin seems to be an effective barrier.

The most significant questions are: how is the aluminium absorbed and by what means does it reach the brain? Our understanding of these processes is poor. Some aluminium appears to be absorbed from the gut by the uptake system which is also used for calcium. In the blood, aluminium is bound to transferrin, the iron transport protein. We have recently found that the sites in the brain where radioactive gallium (a marker for aluminium) is most readily taken up are those which contain a high density of transferrin receptors. So it seems likely that aluminium enters the brain via the system normally used to take up iron. Within cells, iron is stored inside a hollow protein molecule, ferritin. We have recently found that ferritin levels are raised in Alzheimer's disease. It is possible that Alzheimer's disease may involve some inability of the brain to regulate the entry, transport or storage of metal ions. Although this is not the primary disease process, it may be important for secondary degenerative changes to occur.

Aluminosilicate deposits in the brain are of significance in Alzheimer's disease. Let us examine this rather more closely. The aluminium present in the core of senile plaques – perhaps the earliest and most extensive lesion of Alzheimer's disease – is present as highly insoluble aluminosilicate. This complex must be formed at the site of damage. Silicon is present in the body naturally as silicic acid. Silicates and other forms of silicon are not absorbed from the gut. One proposed function of silicic acid is to combine with potentially dangerous metal ions such as aluminium (Al^{3+}) or iron (Fe^{3+}) to prevent oxidative damage to cells. Aluminosilicate deposits may arise as the brain attempts to neutralize aluminium in this way.

To date there are no firm answers as to which factors can contribute to the abnormal accumulation in Alzheimer's disease. In old age many people are in severe negative calcium balance because of reduced dietary intake and impaired calcium absorption due to vitamin D deficiency. A very high proportion (30 per cent) of patients with fractured neck of the femur suffer from severe dementia and a similar proportion show evidence of a milder cognitive impairment. This group of patients has a considerable degree of bone resorption (osteoporosis) due to calcium loss. While demented patients are more likely to fall (and thus to fracture) it is possible that both the osteoporosis and the dementia could reflect a common underlying cause. There is some clinical and biochemical evidence for abnormal calcium handling in Alzheimer's disease and these aspects are being investigated at present.

It is also possible that the deposition of an abnormal protein found around cerebral blood vessels could impair the 'blood-brain barrier' for aluminium and so enable this metal to damage nerve cells. On this hypothesis, Alzheimer's disease would represent the interaction between genetic (the protein) and environmental (aluminium) factors.

Do any of these findings have any bearing on possible treatments or preventative measures for Alzheimer's disease? It is not known whether limiting aluminium intake would help to prevent this disorder or slow down its progression. By the time the symptoms of Alzheimer's disease are obvious, the brain has already undergone extensive degenerative changes. Individuals who wish to limit their exposure to aluminium could do so by using stainless steel or other non-aluminium utensils to cook acidic foods, and by avoiding foods which contain added aluminium (see *Practical pointers*, page 71). Ion exchange filters which remove aluminium from drinking water are commercially available. At the moment there is no effective long-term means to prevent the absorption of aluminium.

Since calcium deficiency may be a possible risk factor, it would be sensible to have a diet rich in calcium (skimmed milk, yogurt, cheese and green vegetables are good sources). However, excessive calcium intake can possibly do harm, notably in people with kidney disorders, so heavy use of calcium supplements should be avoided.

Can we offer any effective treatment for Alzheimer's disease? Recently, it has been claimed that some cholinergic drugs are effective in relieving the early symptoms. One of the most severe biochemical changes in this disorder is the loss in the brain of a chemical messenger, the neurotransmitter substance acetylcholine, which seems important for memory processes. Attempts have been made to replace acetylcholine by increasing the supply of its dietary precursor (choline) or preventing its breakdown by the enzyme acetylcholinesterase (by using drugs such as physostigmine or THA which inhibit the enzyme). The beneficial effects of these drugs reported by some groups have not been found by others workers and the area is controversial at present. Other widely used drugs are based on increasing the cerebral blood flow, but there is now good evidence that this flow is not impaired.

Alzheimer's disease can strike anyone over 40. It is the most common form of dementia which means a progressive decline in the ability to remember, to think and to reason. The start of dementia is very gradual. Mild dementia may reveal itself in slight forgetfulness, apathy, slowness to grasp complex ideas and problems with language, progressing to moderate dementia with disorientation, wandering, loss of memory and double incontinence to severe dementia and helplessness. The outward signs of dementia can be caused by a number of different disorders affecting the brain. Early examination can determine whether the sufferer has a treatable related disorder or actual Alzheimer's disease for which as yet there is no cure. Research has produced helpful medication and nursing techniques to make life more bearable for all concerned.

The Alzheimer's Disease Society which was formed in 1979 was conceived by a retired SRN whose husband had died from the disease. It exists at a national level to foster research, offer counselling, run relieving day centres, increase public awareness of A.D. and other related disorders through the media and fund raising, and produce practical guides to caring. It also offers financial support to sufferers and their families. At a local level the aims are slightly modified. It is the carer and the family that are the prime concern, as caring for a person with the disease can be extremely difficult and stressful at times. Local branches support families by linking them through membership and involving them in the work of the branch, providing information on the aids, services and other resources available, ensuring adequate services are provided for assessment/diagnosis, day care, support at home and residential or hospital care where needed. The address of the Society's Head Office is: 3rd Floor, Bank Buildings, London SW6 1EP (Tel: 01-381 3177) which will provide details of your nearest local contact person or carer's group, Regional office and counselling service.

At risk groups

● **Those working in the aluminium industry and those living in areas surrounding aluminium plants**
Like many industrial related diseases the effects of exposure to toxic substances are not apparent until a number of years later. Whilst those who work directly with aluminium may absorb sizeable quantities, those living in surrounding areas of aluminium plants may also be affected. A health and safety officer working in the aluminium industry described the situation where he worked:

'When aluminium is melted, some of it escapes as vapour. This "melt loss" can be surprisingly large. I can't put a precise figure on it, but I can make an estimate.

'As typical aluminium "Semi-manufacturers" we generated a lot of process scrap and relied on our re-melting facilities for recycling the scrap. Process scrap averaged something like 40 per cent of start-weight. Start weight would have been in the region of 150,000 tonnes per annum, so we were remelting in excess of 50,000 t.p.a. of our own scrap. We also bought in some scrap and we re-melted some raw aluminium too. If we take our scrap figure alone, and consider that over the long term we recovered less than 98 per cent of the molten metal, then we may have been sending 1,000 t.p.a. into the air. You would find the figures easy to check out, since melt-loss was a significant factor in inventory accounting and in our prosperity.

'As for the oil residue, there are probably two main aspects. One is the possibility of there being process oil or burnt process oil on food containing products such as foil, pans, plates, vessels or holloware material. I often wondered whether all of the oil was removed, all of the time. I am not aware of any testing procedures which could have established that, conclusively.

'The annealing furnaces exhausted to atmosphere. We consumed tens of thousands of gallons of light mineral oil, yearly, during aluminium processing. A major contribution to this consumption would have been oil vapour from annealing furnaces. Rolling mill fume extracts would have assisted in this loss. What was not sent out in this way went to our customers on our products. Of course, much of the oil film on products was either desirable, or at least, not significant to its future use in engineering, etc.

'The second and perhaps most interesting aspect of the oil question is the strong likelihood of there being tiny oil inclusion below the surface of rolled aluminium products. I have no idea of what kind of quantities we are thinking of, but the interest lies in the possibility of their release in use, such as during cooking.'

● People with digestive disorders

The causes of digestive disorders are not always apparent, and doctors are left with treating the symptoms. Aluminium-based medicines have been widely used for a number of years to treat digestive disorders. Such compounds as aluminium hydroxide and aluminium hydrate are made into gels, powders, suspensions and tablets and work primarily by neutralizing the acid in the stomach. Due to the large quantities of aluminium used in antacids it is possible for some patients to receive a dose of 1 to 2 grammes daily. They have been until now seen as a safe and easy way to treat digestive disorders. Perhaps reconsideration is necessary when looking at the most recent data on the possible long term effects of consuming sizeable quantities of aluminium.

● Premature babies

Babies born before they are carried full term need special care and treatment. Their kidneys are not completely developed and therefore are not fully capable of excreting poisonous substances. In some cases premature babies have to be fed intravenously. Before it was realized that aluminium could be toxic to the body some premature babies actually died from aluminium poisoning. Today this does not occur because the intravenous fluid is carefully monitored for aluminium.

● Elderly people

As people get older the kidneys become generally less efficient. Elderly people become increasingly at risk from taking in aluminium because their kidneys cannot excrete the aluminium as well as they have previously done. As there is no routine measuring of aluminium levels in the blood it is sensible to follow the practical pointers as laid out at the end of this chapter.

● **The general public**

Are exposed to aluminium in the ways already outlined e.g., through treated water, aluminium foil, utensils, etc. It could depend on how an individual's body handles aluminium as to whether he or she develops symptoms of poisoning. As there are no widespread methods available for screening for the defective chromosome 21 nor monitoring of aluminium levels in the general public, it is difficult to accurately assess how much one is at risk. Following the practical pointers may be sufficient but with more work yet to be carried out we cannot be absolutely certain. It is generally accepted that as one gets older one's memory fades, concentration levels become lower and one's ability to reason becomes less agile. The question is: 'Is this simply due to natural ageing *or* could exposure to high levels of aluminium over the years be a contributory factor?' It is going to be very difficult to answer this question, especially as the attitude at present among doctors is 'What can you expect at your age?'

If aluminium were to be implicated in pre-senile dementia and other forms of dementia then screening should become routine. For those who have accumulated high levels of aluminium in their blood, an annual blood cleansing session could prevent the onset of symptoms.

Practical pointers

● For those of you who regularly use antacids, whether prescribed by your doctor or bought over the counter at a chemists, ask for a different type of antacids, one that contains magnesium trisilicate only and is free from all aluminium.

● If you have been using aluminium-based medication for some time and suspect you are suffering from de-calcification effects often experienced by those exposed to excessive doses of aluminium, then a diet high in calcium rich foods may be of some benefit. Foods that are rich in calcium are: milk and milk products e.g., cheese; sardines and other fish where the bones are eaten; fresh vegetables, especially peas; watercress; fruits such as dried figs and peaches; and nuts such as almonds and brazils. All could be included in a good balanced diet to replace any lost calcium.

● The level of aluminium in your drinking water will largely depend upon where it comes from. If it flows through peaty areas it may naturally have a brownish tinge which is removed by your local water authority during the treatment of the water by generally using aluminium sulphate. This discoloration should theoretically be removed during the filtration processes. As already explained, drinking water does contain significant quantities of aluminium. A water filtration system fitted to your domestic supply reduces your exposure to aluminium. The type that will remove aluminium is relatively expensive to install, and works on a principle called reverse osmosis. It needs regular maintenance in changing the filters. (See nitrates for fuller details of water filters available for use in the home.)

● Aluminium has been extensively used for household utensils for many years. Although there is no definite proof that these are harmful to health it is a good idea to replace them with stainless steel equivalents (see packaging materials for further details on aluminium).

● If there is a choice between using fresh vegetables and canned foods always choose the former. All canned foods have large quantities of lead and even the new cans that do not use lead solder, are usually made of aluminium.

Nitrates

Nitrates are chemicals that occur naturally in water and the soil. They are also applied as fertilizers to the ground and used as preservatives in food manufacture for making ham, canned meats, etc. Much has been written about the adverse health effects of nitrates but sadly to date no real change has taken place.

Water and nitrates

Certain areas of Britain have higher levels of nitrates in their water than others. There are background levels of nitrates found everywhere both in soil and water. However, the pockets of high nitrate concentration which are found in water are mainly attributed to intensive farming methods which include the use of large scale applications of fertilizers and manure. All fertilizers contain a percentage of nitrate and, as with everything that is put on the ground, some seeps through the soil and finds its way into streams, water courses and reservoirs and ultimately into the drinking water. Continued exposure to raised levels of nitrate in water may well cause health problems.

We assume our water is of a quality safe to drink, but can we really know? The guidelines of 1985 set down by the EEC and WHO state that drinking water should not contain more than 45-50 mg of nitrates per litre (Figures taken from N. Dudley: *Nitrates in Food and Water* – London Food Commission). However, it has been found that 70 UK water supplies exceed 50 mg per litre of water; over 1,000,000 people are regularly supplied with water over the agreed level of nitrates daily, according to Nigel Dudley.

If nitrate reduction was carried out routinely the cost would be borne by the water authority and then passed on to the consumer. We can assume therefore that for the consumer to have an acceptable quality of water he or she will be called upon to indirectly subsidize the fertilizer industry, the polluters of our water supply. Although to actually identify the polluter is very difficult and prosecution would be almost impossible, the principle that the polluter should pay seems to be totally ignored.

You will see that vegetables contribute the largest amount of nitrate to the foods you eat. They should not normally have this high nitrate content; naturally they would take up just enough nitrate from the soil for their own use to make into body-building proteins. If they are given too much nitrate in the way of fertilizers, the following can happen:

● They do not have the capacity to use up all the nitrates and so the excess is left in the tissues of the plant.

● If harvesting is done while the plant is still growing and trying to use up its supply of nitrates, there will be a significant amount of nitrate still left in the harvested vegetables.

Nitrates in water

Water – depending on your area	Weekly intake in milligrams
low	100
medium	500
high	750
very high	1,000

Nitrates in foods

Product	Weekly intake in milligrams
Meat products	37
Milk	87
Cheese	5
Vegetables	224
Potatoes	63
Total	**416** milligrams per week

Nitrates found in some vegetables in Britain
Milligram per kilogram

Product – Vegetable	Average value milligrams
Spinach	2,056
Cabbage	258
Cauliflower	186
Carrots	120
Potatoes	83

Reference: N. Dudley: *Nitrates in Food and Water* –London Food Commission

- In growing crops in greenhouses during the winter, where there is reduced light, nitrates are unable to be converted into body-building proteins and high levels of residual nitrates are found in winter grown greenhouse vegetables.

- Modern high-yielding varieties of crops are developed especially to grow in nitrate-rich soils. These crops have the ability to accumulate large reserves of nitrates in their cells. The highest nitrate levels are generally found in leaves and stems and therefore in such vegetables as lettuce, spinach and cabbage. Nitrates are found to a lesser extent in root crops such as carrots and potatoes and lower levels are found in fruit.

Milk and nitrates

Dairy farmers often use fertilizers to encourage luscious green pasture land for their animals to graze on. As we have already established, these fertilizers have a high nitrate content. The grass takes up the nitrates while growing, the animal eats the grass, the grass takes up even more nitrates from the soil and the cow ends up having a nitrate rich diet – further compounded by the animal taking in even more nitrates through its drinking water supply.

The final result is that the animal produces milk with a nitrate content and as most people consume an average of one pint per day they will therefore be receiving a significant amount of nitrate regularly.

Meat and nitrates

Although nitrates are not a desirable part of our diet, we have to accept that if they were abolished certain foods would also disappear. These foods include bacon, gammon, ham and various cuts of cured pork e.g., streaky, back, slipper, hock and hand. This is because during the process of making cured pork nitrates became an essential ingredient. Without it, there would be no pink colouration or the characteristic flavour associated with cured pork products.

At the moment nitrate is an essential preservative in many tinned or processed meats e.g., corned beef, paté and sausages, because these foods are an ideal place for the growth of a lethal bacteria called *clostridium botulinium*. The nitrates ensure that the bacteria do not have the chance to produce their deadly toxin.

The lack of research and development in the food industry into less hazardous alternatives to nitrates has led to their routine use. It has been suggested that by using ascorbic acid (Vitamin C) and sorbic acid the use of nitrates and nitrites could be reduced considerably. (See the changing of nitrates into nitrites below for a fuller explanation of the difference between nitrates and nitrites.) nitrites.)

The consumer needs to alert the food manufacturers to this fact and urge them to carry out more research into the whole area of nitrate use. If nitrates and nitrites were removed and suitable substitutes with a lower toxicity level were used it would go a long way to reducing our overall nitrate and nitrite consumption.

Health hazards and risk factors

We are all consuming regular and significant quantities of nitrates, and because the government is not, in spite of public concern, in the forseeable future intending to change its policies and revise legislation in this area we are likely to see an even greater increase in the future. This in turn has meant that the consumer is taking a keener interest in the nitrate problem and the possible effects from it on his/her health and will be looking for ways to reduce risk factors.

The changing of nitrates into nitrites

Nitrates in themselves are relatively harmless, unless one was to consume an enormous amount, because they are quickly eliminated by the body through the kidneys. The main health hazard to the consumer is where the *nitrate* changes into *nitrite* which occurs by reduction. This reduction takes place by means of microbial nitrate-reductases, and this occurs in four ways:

- originating in the stomach/intestine

- originating in the mouth

- from poor storage of foodstuffs

● from poor storage and reheating of prepared foods.

Nitrites to nitrosamines

To complete the story of how nitrates become a nitrosamine and ultimately a health hazard we have to consider the following. Nitrosamines are formed as a result of secondary or tertiary amines or amides with nitrites. This chemical reaction usually takes place at a pH of 2 or 3. However, the presence of the catalysts thiocyanate or halagenoids allows it to take place at even lower ph levels. These conditions we have discussed are to be found in the human stomach. The consumer who smokes will have thiocyanate concentrations three or four times greater than a non-smoker. Smokers are more at risk than non-smokers, and can have build-ups of nitrosamines in their stomach.

There is some evidence to suggest that nitrosamines under certain circumstances may cause stomach cancer. There also are indications that nitrosamines could cause oesophageal (food pipe) cancer, but to date there has been little or no research carried out.

Stomach cancer

We discovered earlier in the chapter that the consumer takes in significant amounts of nitrates from vegetables, milk and meat. It would, however, be unwise of the consumer to reduce or stop eating these foods in the hope of reducing the risk of developing stomach cancer.

We know firstly that stomach cancer has been on the decline in Britain for over the past 50 years. This is believed to be the result of safer food storage, in particular refrigeration, and faster distribution methods. Food distribution methods have made a particularly significant contribution by reducing the consumer's exposure to trichothecenes and other carcinogenic mycotoxins.

Blue baby syndrome (methaemoglobinaemia cyanosis)

The blue baby syndrome is a potentially fatal condition. It comes about through consuming high nitrite levels which cause the *oxidation of haemoglobin*. The blue discoloration of the skin is caused by a lack of oxygen in the blood. Babies under the age of three months seem to be particularly susceptible to this condition.

This is because their enzyme system is not mature enough to reverse this process as it would be in adults. To make matters worse a baby's stomach has a ph conducive to the build-up of nitrate-reducing bacteria. The encouraging news was that this condition was studied and the appropriate changes made and there has not been a single case since 1972.

A warning on nitrates comes from Nigel Dudley's report, *Nitrates in Food and Water* produced by the London Food Commission: 'It must also be remembered that environmental levels of nitrates have only risen really significantly in the past couple of decades so that their medical effects may not be fully apparent yet. Meanwhile, nitrate levels in water are still rising, and this rise may become even more acute still in the future. If nitrates are implicated in stomach cancer the evidence may not yet be available, but may turn up in populations in the future.'

Practical pointers

● Food manufacturers, farmers and water authorities are at present not concerned enough about the possible health hazards of nitrates to take any concrete steps towards reducing the amounts of nitrate in our food and water. Because of this it is up to you to ensure that those concerned are fully aware of your feelings and opinions on the matter. As well as giving your opinions you also want assurances that your comments will be acted upon. This is usually a long and arduous task as such correspondence is often ignored. However, if sufficient people make their feelings known, the weight of public pressure can force major changes in policy.

The recent public concern about additives immediately springs to mind; during the past two years we have seen a revolution taking place in the supermarkets. Suddenly the words 'additive free' have become synonymous with quality and desirability. People had been demanding additive-free foods for some time, and the manufacturers, because they saw the possibility of increased trade, finally bowed submissively to the demands of the consumer. The consumer should always remember the purchasing power he commands and the power of refusal to buy that is also his.

To ensure good public health, good quality products and a safe water supply you should continue to make known to the food and water producers your views and concerns about present production methods in the light of recent research and ask them to act upon it. The producers should be expected to provide as well thought out a product as possible with continual reviewing and constant update of production methods where necessary or else risk losing your custom.

The consumer should continually assess all food and water products and where deficiencies are felt to occur should as soon as time allows make comment to those who are in a position to make change. For those of you who are unfamiliar with such procedures below are some address and guidelines to follow. (Other relevant addresses and guidelines will appear in other chapters.)

Making your opinions known

The value of your personal opinion should never be undervalued. Do not feel overwhelmed by contacting such people as MPs, supermarkets and your local water authority. To help you a sample letter is included here for you to use. This can obviously be altered to suit your own requirements, but ensures that you ask the right questions. Your letter will be more effective if you write to your local MP at the House of Commons rather than to a Minister. Letters direct are dealt with by civil servants and do not reach the appropriate person.

A list of addresses follow which have been chosen as the appropriate people to contact on this issue.

- **Your local MP's name,**
C/o The House of Commons
London SW1A 0AA

- **The Ministry of Agriculture, Food and Fisheries**
Horseferry Road,
London
SW1P 2AE

- **The Department of Health and Social Security (DHSS)**
Chief Medical Officer,
Alexander Fleming House,
Elephant and Castle
London SE1 6BY

- **Water Authorities**

Use your local telephone directory or obtain the address from your water rate bill.

- **National Farmers' Union**

Environmental Matters Department,
4 St Mary's Place,
Stamford,
Lincs PE9 2DN

- **Food manufacturers and supermarkets**

Look at the label of the product and check if nitrate and/or nitrite appear(s). If so, write to the public relations department of the particular food company concerned, using the sample letter below as a guide (you will find the company's Head Office address on the packet/container). It may also be of interest and benefit to write directly to the local supermarket(s) to find out its/their policy on nitrates.

Sample letter for nitrates

(To: Food Manufacturers; National Farmers' Union; Water Authorities; MPs; Ministry of Agriculture, Food and Fisheries; the DHSS)

Dear _____

I am concerned about the levels of nitrates in my diet, because of the present uncertainties as to their possible health risks.

I would like to know your views on the nitrate situation and your present policy towards nitrates generally. Do you have any plans to actively reduce nitrate levels?

Yours faithfully.

Extra notes to farmers and food manufacturers

Are you actively looking for alternatives to nitrates in your food production?

If you cannot satisfy me as a consumer that you are trying to lower nitrate levels, I shall have no alternative but to buy organic foodstuffs.

Extra notes to MPs

I would also like to know your party's views on the nitrate problem.

As you are my only means of making my opinions known and heard, I must urge you to seriously undertake to speak out on my behalf on this serious issue.

I expect you to continuously raise this issue until we see lowered levels of nitrates acceptable to all consumers.

Extra notes to the Ministry of Agriculture, Food and Fisheries and the Department of Health and Social Security (DHSS)

Do you have any plans to carry out research into the health hazards of nitrates?

Is the question of nitrates in the food chain a high priority?

From the data made available to you, how much of it is put into practical use?

● To stop smoking will take you out of an at-risk group. It must however be realized that there is a time lapse between giving up and acquiring the same risk factor as a non-smoker because the stomach needs time to reduce the thiocyanate concentrations.

● Certain foodstuffs have a high nitrite content. These are leaf and some root vegetables, medicines, cured meat, milk, grains, eggs, beer, wine and finally seafood with a very high nitrate content. If they mix with the amines that are always present in the stomach the risk of nitrosamines developing is much greater. Because an acid medium inhibits this chemical reaction it would be prudent to mix such foods with foods rich in Vitamin C and Vitamin E.

Foods rich in Vitamin C are: red and green peppers; sprouts; blackcurrants; strawberries; citrus fruits; tomatoes.

Foods rich in Vitamin E are: Beemax; Wheatbran; Allbran; muesli; Weetabix; rich fruit cake; eggs especially yolks; margarine and oils especially polyunsaturated margarine; cod liver oil; vegetable oil especially wheatgerm, safflower and sunflower; tinned fish; tomato and tomato products; asparagus; parsley; avocado pears; hedgerow blackberries; nuts especially almonds, brazils, hazelnuts and peanuts.

To give a clearer idea of how to combine nitrate rich foods and phenolic compounds (Vitamin C and E) that inhibit the chemical reaction here are several meal plans with the inhibiting foods in italics.

Breakfast 1
> *Fresh orange juice*   grilled bacon and *grilled tomatoes*
>   fried egg
>   wholemeal roll

Breakfast 2
> *grapefruit segments*   home-made *muesli* with added *wheatgerm, chopped apple* and *strawberries*

Snack 1
> *Asparagus* soup
> pâté sandwich with wholemeal bread and *mixed pepper salad*
> glass red wine
> one *orange*

Snack 2
> salami pizza with *mixed avocado salad*
> milk shake made with *fresh fruit*

Main meal 1
> seafood platter with *lemon wedges*
> **or**
> grilled steak with *side salad*
> glass of beer
> *fresh fruit salad*

Main meal 2
> steak and kidney pie
> *mashed potatoes*
> peas
> *blackberry* crumble and custard

● As some vegetables have a significant nitrate content the consumer could as alternatives either (a) choose vegetables grown organically or (b) increase fruit consumption and reduce consumption of leaf and some root vegetables ensuring that overall nutrient consumption is in no way affected. To reduce nitrate consumption here are some suggested alternatives:

have less of	spinach cabbage cauliflower carrots potatoes	**have more of**	green beans, butter beans, peas, green and red pepper macaroni, pasta, rice

● As a general guide eating fewer prepared meat products could also help reduce overall nitrate consumption. The products in question are pâtés; meat loaves; potted beef; bacon; ham; gammon (cured meats); salami; continental meats; pork pies; veal and ham pie; hot dogs; sausages; beefburgers; ready made meat meals, etc.
Some of these products are available with the additives reduced. However, in certain cases no alternative can be found.

● It is possible but not for certain, to produce certain conditions for a build-up of bacteria to occur in the mouth that have the potential to alter nitrates into more harmful substances. To ensure this does not add to the nitrate problem good mouth hygiene is essential. The cleaning of teeth, removal of particles of food with floss and the use of antiseptic mouth washes are all preventive measures that can be routinely carried out. This in conjunction with regular visits to a dentist and/or hygienist will ensure that the risk is reduced. This is equally as important for children as well as adults.

● The consumer expects the foods he or she buys to have been suitably stored and handled and significant improvements have taken place in this area in recent years. As a result of this market trading in food of unknown origins is on the decline. Foods today quickly pass through the distribution chain and are sold to the consumer within days and in some cases even hours of being bought. 'Sell by' dates ensure the freshness of food particularly in the case of perishable foodstuffs. This overall improvement in distribution and food management has resulted in reduced contamination and deterioration of foodstuffs ensuring that nitrates do not have time to make their presence felt, by causing ill-health.

● Purchase perishables from shops with a rapid turnover.

● Avoid foodstuffs with an unknown history – even if they do seem good buys.

● At one time death from food poisoning or poor hygenic conditions was fairly common. It has only been reduced since the consumer has had ready access to antiseptics, antibiotics, hot water and improved housing conditions. Methods of food preservation and storage have improved with refrigerators and deep freezers becoming commonplace. The consumer feels often that he can relax because he does not feel at risk. Sadly this is not the case as bacteria are always changing and it is still therefore very important to maintain good standards of hygiene and cleanliness. One of the main risks from nitrates in the home is in the reheating of food, especially meat dishes. However, this does seem to be becoming less of a problem now because of the use of microwave ovens where foods can be kept refrigerated until required, then reheated for the allotted time and then consumed without delay.

By considering all these factors the consumer can reduce risk from nitrates considerably.

Water filters that can remove nitrates

Manufacturer	Type	Removes	Cost Initial	Annual
Fileder Systems Ltd 50 Old Road, Wateringbury, Kent ME18 5PL	**Type A** plumbed-in attachment on tap	chlorine organic taints – sediment	£215	£5
	Type B plumbed-in attachment on tap	up to 90 per cent – fluoride, nitrate, sodium – but also useful minerals, iron, calcium, magnesium, potassium	£75	£40
La Source de Vie P.O. Box 66, Chichester, W. Sussex PO18 9HH	"Mayrei 2000" attachment on taps	mercury, copper and chlorine 90 per cent lead and cadmium 50-70 per cent sediment 80 per cent nitrate 20 per cent	£10 approximately monthly	
Food Watch Butts Pond Industrial Estate Sturminster Newton, Dorset DT10 1AZ		Have a range of water filters available. For the removal of nitrates, fluorides and aluminium, the most difficult minerals to remove, there is now a reverse osmosis domestic system available from the States. This is the method used to produce dialysis grade water for renal patients. It produces approximately 2½ gallons of pure water daily. Available at a reasonable price through Food Watch.		
Arbour Tech Limited The Arbour Farm Kingsland Leominster, Herefordshire HR6 9SF. Tel no 056881 8840	Full Range Domestic and Commercial Water Treatment Equipment	Reverse osmosis removes toxins and produces pure water • will also offer water testing facilities	From £60 for basic domestic model upwards depending on water treatment system chosen	

Other water filtrations methods offering varying degrees of performance

Manufacturer	Type	Removes	Cost Initial	Annual
Amsoil Whitehaven Products, Leigh Road, Bradford-on-Avon Wilts BA15 2RS	Aquabrite plumbed in below sink	organics mercury – most of *not* lead fluoride type supplied	£135+	£25-30
Brita UK Ltd Yssel House, Queen's Road, Horsham Surrey KT12 5NE	Jug from individual cup to 2 litre	lead – 100 per cent copper – organics chlorine – 90 per cent cadmium – mercury up to 70 per cent *not* fluoride	£3–£12	£12–£24
Fairey Industrial Ceramics Ltd, Filleybrooks, Stone Staffs ST15 0PU	NFU and NHNS plumbed in above sink	mercury, copper and chlorine 90 per cent lead, cadmium – 50-70 per cent sediment – 80 per cent nitrate – 20 per cent	£10+ monthly	
Fospur Ltd, Dudley Rd, Kingswinford DY6 8XF	Safari **AB1/C** or **AB1/F** incl. tap plumbed in below sink	Suspended matter chlorine detergents organic taints asbestos	£99 £160	£46 £40

Packaging materials

It is a long time since the consumer bought food wrapped in greaseproof paper which was then put into a paper bag bearing adverts for tea or oranges. People expect the packaging of foodstuffs to be attractive, hygienic and easy to handle, and with the help of modern technological developments the food industry has kept pace with consumer demand.

Plastics

Much of the packaging used today is plastic or has a plastic coating of some kind; even glass bottles have plastic caps or plastic seals. Plastic is popular becomes it comes in a variety of forms and is light and often transparent. The product inside can be seen and the customer can feel satisfied that the food cannot be handled and therefore to a certain extent remains hygienically fresh. Most plastic for packaging is made from 'polymeric' materials such as polyethylene and polyvinylchloride (PVC). Depending on the characteristics required plastics can vary immensely e.g., for a more flexible plastic one would add more plasticizer, derived as a by-product from the petro-chemical industry.

Packaging materials in use today

- Plastics. These come in a variety of forms: PVC; transparent; rigid containers; polystyrene trays and containers; perspex; teflon; polythene; flexible plastic packaging material (clingfilm)

- Glass

- Aluminium foil

- Cardboard covered with wax or plastic – tetra packs

- Paper

Food packaging regulations in Britain stipulate that packaging materials must not transfer their constituents to foods in amounts that might be harmful to human health or could cause deterioration in the food itself. It is not generally known that some plastics are not of food grade; even worse there is no symbol or markings that indicate whether it is safe for food use. This is clearly confusing for the consumer. There has been an EEC proposal to label plastic materials safe for use with food but it would be impractical to label every item made from plastic. Following on from this there would have to be strict checks to ensure that manufacturers kept to the EEC directives – a very difficult task!

The most recent plastic packaging material to come under scrutiny is flexible plastic packaging material (clingfilm). Results taken from a study carried out by the National Cancer Institute in the USA (1980) showed that the plasticizers used in its manufacture DEHA (diethylhexyl adipate) and DEHP (diethylhexl phthalate) carried definite links with cancer in rats and mice. Since actual figures have not been quoted it is difficult to assess the true implications of these findings. However these plasticizers are lipophilic (fat loving) and are therefore much more likely to migrate into fat rich foods such as bacon, ham, salami, cheese, butter, margarine, pâté and fish. The use of this plastic material has been actively encouraged in many microwave cookbooks and microwave cookery programmes on television for covering foods to prevent drying out or to stop food splattering over the inside of the microwave oven. Since 1986 MAFF has not recommended the use of clingfilm for lining dishes and close wrapping of food, and it is continuing to investigate the matter.

Practical pointers

● Use only rigid plastic containers that are advertised for use with food e.g., Tupperware.

● Do not use buckets to ferment your beer or wine in as they are not made from food grade plastics and dangerous chemicals can seep into the liquid, especially from the coloured type.

● Wrap food in greaseproof paper before placing in a plastic container especially if it is rich in fat or if it will have to spend many hours in the container before being eaten.

● Use covered casserole dishes, Pyrex, china dishes or dampened kitchen towels in microwave cooking.

● There is a clingfilm available by post from Foodwatch called Lexfilm. It is plasticizer free, and has two percent of vegetable derived additives added to ensure the correct cling and breathing properties. It comes in 150 metres/30 cm roll and is reasonably priced. It is not suitable, however, for use in microwaves.

● Remove all foods from plastic containers as soon as possible after purchasing to reduce the amount of contact time between foodstuff and container.

● Where possible, use china, glass, Pyrex, stoneware or earthenware with a glaze to store foods with a high fat content. This is to reduce the amount of contact time.

● Ask at your supermarket or health food shop for goods to be packaged in greaseproof paper and paper bags. As there is no reasonable way of knowing whether the plastics used in the majority of packaging materials are of food grade it is prudent to ask for an alternative.

Paper

Because paper is made from natural raw materials we have yet to discover whether it, too, presents any cause for concern. It does, however, have limitations: it rips easily, it allows spilt foods and grease to seep through and foods often stick to it. Plastics overcome these problems, but as we are now finding out, at a price.

However, paper does allow food to 'breathe' and in the interests of good health and hygiene paper seems to come out on top.

Practical pointers

● Paper production needs raw materials and as these can be costly, the need to recycle is vital. So if you have a recycling service do make every effort to use it.

Cardboard

Cardboard by itself is a useful packaging material – often printed with a logo or serving suggestion giving some indication of the product it contains. Cardboard packaging doesn't, however, allow the customer to see the actual product, a problem which is often overcome by inserting a plastic window somewhere on the container. In some cases cardboard is used for foods people do not want to see anyway, such as breakfast cereals. One of the cardboard's shortcomings is that it cannot be successfully used for liquids, a problem now overcome by coating the cardboard with wax, plastics or foil. Coatings have changed the way some products are sold. For example, the boxes can be made sterile, known commercially as Tetra Packs, so that liquids such as soup, milk or desserts can be packaged without the use of preservatives or heat treatment that might impair the flavour and make the product unacceptable to some customers. Bearing in mind what has been said so far, it would be prudent to purchase goods that have wax linings as opposed to plastic or foil linings.

Practical pointers

● When you are presented with a choice, purchase goods that

have not been in contact with plastic or foil-coated cardboard.

● If you have a recycling service do make an effort to use it.

Glass

Glass is a very versatile and pleasing method of packaging food. It has only one drawback as far as the manufacturer is concerned: it adds cost to the product, in some cases as much as ten per cent. However, if recycling was organized on a national scale this cost could be reduced but until such times as recycling becomes an accepted part of the food manufacturing industry these high costs will remain.

Practical pointers

● If you have a bottle bank or local recycling service make an effort to use and promote it.

Aluminium foil

Aluminium foil has been an accepted packaging material in the home and commercially for a number of years. It is extremely useful and is used extensively for cooking meat, wrapping sandwiches, and covering odd bits of food in and keeping them moist in the fridge. In most households you would find aluminium foil somewhere, and you would undoubtedly find aluminium used in other kitchen utensils – saucepans, pressure cookers, roasting tins, bakeware and tea pots.

Until recently we have used aluminium freely but has this been very wise? There have been a number of reports that after long term low level exposure to aluminium it can destroy the brain cells resulting in loss of memory (see page 63).

Aluminium foil, when made, is rolled very thinly and to ensure that the rollers glide easily during this rolling process, industrial grade mineral oil is used. According to the manufacturers this should not constitute a health hazard as the foil is heated to a high temperature and in theory the mineral oil burns off. However, no matter how careful one is there will always be a small percentage of mineral oil residue remaining. You can sometimes detect this when your foil has a greasy feel to it.

Acid foods leach out aluminium, and so does tannin. Therefore any acidic foods wrapped in aluminium foil will be found to have an increased aluminium content when left for a number of hours.

Although no one as yet has restricted the use of aluminium there are a number of practical pointers one can follow to reduce risk.

Practical pointers

● Discontinue using aluminium saucepans and cookware. Stainless steel and good grade pure cast iron are sensible alternatives.

● When choosing a tea pot china, earthenware, porcelain or stainless steel are good choices.

● Remove foods as soon as possible from foil packaging so reducing contact time.

● If you wish to use foil, wrap foods, especially those that are acidic, in greaseproof paper first.

● For roasting meat use a meat brick made from earthenware, alternatively make up a flour and water dough and cover your joint of meat in this simple dough and cook as usual.

CHAPTER 3

The food chain connection

Fish

Fish is considered a healthy food and we are encouraged to eat more by nutritionists. On average, the British eat fish about once a week. To help in the prevention of heart disease we are advised to eat fish three or four times a week. This is a way of reducing fat intake, but may also increase the risk of exposure to pollutants.

Sea fish, which includes cod, haddock, halibut, herrings, mackerel, shell fish, etc., live in an environment which is constantly being polluted. Some say that the sea is able to cope with this pollution, but who is monitoring how well it is coping? And how much more can it take? Environmental groups like Greenpeace and Friends of the Earth actively seek to improve the quality of sea water. This water has to contend with the dumping of nuclear waste, untreated sewage, industrial waste (via rivers), waste from ships, oil and toxic chemicals. Some seas are more polluted than others and some have 'black holes' – small pockets where no life exists at all. Should these black holes become larger it is possible that they could seriously threaten the fishing industry.

Fresh water fish especially the products of intensive fish farming e.g., trout and salmon are potentially even more exposed to pollutants. Most rivers are polluted to some extent by pesticide and fertilizer 'run-off' from farms and industrial plants. In addition, factory farmed fish are given doses of antibiotics to prevent the spread of disease in their tanks. As the conditions under which these animals are kept become more restricted they show signs of environmental stress and so become ill more frequently and pass on illness more readily.

Bread and cereals

Cereals of all kinds are part of our daily diet and we are encouraged to eat more as part of a healthy living campaign. Wholemeal products are promoted in preference to their refined counterparts; this seems most commendable until you consider the fact that it is the bran part of a cereal grain that actually absorbs most of the pesticides. Therefore, by eating wholegrain products grown by agrochemical methods you will be consuming considerably more pesticide residues than you would by eating white flour products. It would, on the other hand, not be sensible to return to the fibreless white flour products. The answer is, of course, actively to seek wholegrain organic products that display the Soil Association Symbol. This also applies to fruit and vegetables for by eating their skins to obtain more fibre you are also consuming an increased dose of residues. Again the alternative is not to give up eating vegetables, but either to peel them or buy organically grown ones.

This evidence is to be found in the Report of the Working Party on Pesticide Residues (1982 to 1985), page 22:

'A study commenced in April 1984 of residues in retail cereal products, especially on those made from wheat. It is well established that residues of insecticides applied to wheat tend to be found in the *bran* component, and therefore emphasis will be placed on bran and bran based products. Other important products e.g., brown bread will be investigated at a later date.'

Some figures will highlight the point even further (1984). From 51 samples of wholemeal flour, 15 were found to have a residue content. In the bran samples, 28 of the 65 were found to have a residue content, and finally 7 out of 66 bran-based breakfast cereals were found to have a residue content. The residues were of an organophosphorous insecticide origin.

The production of cereals has been so successful that we are now able to export them. With the use of pesticides, fertilizers and selective strains of plants we have also accumulated an embarrassing surplus that now has to be stored. If the quality of the grain is not maintained during storage, any pest infestation obviously reduces storage time and the value of the grain. To overcome this a selection of organophosphorus insecticides and fumigants are used. MAFF have monitored the levels in the stored grains and state in their report that no organophosphorus or organochlorine compounds were found. However, two from the 50 samples tested for fumigants were found to have levels above the Codex Alimentarius Commission MRL's.*

* This is an international committee who decide on the amounts of residues allowed to be left in food.

Poultry and eggs

Chicken is promoted as a healthy food and consumption has increased in recent years because it has become more economic to produce. This decrease in price has been made possible by the use of growth promoters within the factory farming of poultry. The fact that poultry can be from egg to table within eight weeks means that yearly output is enormous, and costs are low, resulting in big profits from operating on an intensive farming basis.

Keeping poultry in a free range situation is not always practicable. Most therefore are kept inside either in a deep litter or box. Feed is cereal based and may therefore contain traces of pesticides, artificial colourants to produce bright yellow yolks and antibiotics to prevent the spread of infection. Antibiotics can also be considered types of growth promoters because poultry free from disease will grow more rapidly. This is a matter of interpretation. As a general rule, contaminants found in poultry will also be found in their eggs e.g., feeding bright yellow food dye will produce an egg with an artificially bright yellow yolk.

Wood shavings are often used for poultry bedding and it is very likely that birds will become contaminated by the preservative used on the wood. MAFF found that 30 per cent of all egg laying hens in the UK are reared on wood shavings and two per cent spend their entire life on wood shavings. MAFF have looked particularly at the level of pentachlorophenol (wood preservative) in the livers and eggs of poultry reared on wood shavings. They found that the chemical did migrate into the birds and hence into their eggs. Figures quoted are 0.4 milligrams per kilo of chicken livers and 0.08 milligrams per kilo of chicken eggs.

One 'real' egg producer advertises on his egg boxes that his eggs are free from antibiotics and hormones. When asked why he does so, he said: 'The housewife wants unadultered foods and I can sell my eggs at a premium. My aim in business is to give the consumer what he or she wants.'

Meat

Meat may have a pesticide content because of the contaminated foods animals are given and also from dipping in organophosphates. MAFF has found detectable quantities of pesticide residues in animal feed. It has also found pesticide residues in imported meat products.

Intensive farming techniques involve the use of antibiotics to restrict the spread of infection. Therefore antibiotics may be present in meat, some of which are the same as those given to man. The consequent possibility of man becoming resistant to life-saving antibiotics is now of concern.

Milk and milk products – cheese, yogurt, butter

If meat can contain residues of pesticides then we can assume that milk will also have a residue content, especially as milk has a fat content and many pesticides dissolve in fat. If milk and milk products are contaminated it should be of concern because of the quantity consumed by us all.

Growth promoters can be used to speed up milk production. One of interest at the moment is Bovine somatotrophin (BST). A literal translation of BST is cow cell growth. It is a protein hormine naturally produced in the cow. There is a relationship between naturally occuring BST levels in a cow and the amount of milk it produces. A farmer may look upon BST as an opportunity to reduce his number of cows but still maintain his levels of milk production. BST is given by injection and is produced synthetically. In these times of over-production, it does seem ludicrous to be marketing such products. What really needs to happen is for farmers to produce enough milk to fulfil our needs, and improve the quality of that by reducing residues and marketing more organic dairy produce. Although some may say that we are already absorbing minute doses of BST with no ill effects, we do not know what effect increased levels may have on human health.

Antibiotics are a regular treatment for mastitis and the farmer should throw away all milk from treated cows. The Milk Marketing Board checks the milk on arrival and performs a set of routine tests which include looking for antibiotics.

If they are found the farmer is heavily penalized. Theoretically there should be no antibiotic residues as they would interfere with the making of cheese and yogurt where bacteria are an essential ingredient.

Fruit and vegetables

Fruit and vegetable consumption is steadily increasing due to obvious nutritional benefits and the wide variety of each now readily available. Because of an increase in vegetarianism, peas, beans and lentils are now more widely used. However, in tests they have been found to contain organochlorine residues. Although generally low this is of possible concern to those who eat pulses as their main source of protein.

The concern is the vegetable quality and the possibility of pesticide residues being present in the vegetables eaten daily. The farmer uses a combination of many different chemicals on the ground – herbicides and insecticides are the main ones. It is essential during their use that instructions are carried out very carefully. For example, some need an interval of time between spraying and harvesting of crops. This time lapse varies considerably and there is no way of checking whether crops have been picked early. Spraying of vegetable crops is routine and some farmers use aerial spraying for convenience. The drawback with aerial spraying is that other crops, animals, waterways and possibly people can be contaminated by poor working practices.

The MAFF report of the Working Party on Pesticide Residues 1982 to 1985 states that 648 samples of UK produced vegetables were analysed of which 184 (28 per cent) contained residues at concentrations greater than the set limits. From imported produce 1,001 samples were analysed and 524 contained residues above the set limits. MAFF states that such levels should not be considered a hazard to consumer health!

Fruit and vegetables may be contaminated while still growing but are also subjected to pesticide treatment after harvest. They may be sprayed with chemicals to preserve their colour and quality during storage and transportation. The MAFF Working Party are continuing surveillance on post-harvest treatment to provide more up-to-date information.

Water

Water plays a vital part in the food chain connection because it is the one commodity that we all use. It is because water has such an important part to play in our lives that its purity is so important. Any contamination will permeate through the *whole* food chain, although it is very difficult to prove that the water itself is the actual contaminant. Most consumers assume their water is of a high quality and is constantly checked by government bodies. When you have considered and reflected upon the information available, you will probably be far from satisfied about the purity of your water supply. The next move is to complain (see nitrates, page 72).

Rain water was once considered to be good for the complexion.

Considering the present levels of contamination, would this still be true? Contamination of rain water has worldwide implications. The far-reaching effects of Chernobyl provide a good example. Rain water contaminated with radiation has found its way into the food chain by its absorption into grass, meat, milk, vegetables, fish and ultimately into man. This type of residue contamination exists all over the world. We shall not know the full consequences of Chernobyl for many years to come.

Another example of the way contamination can spread is through the industrial production of sulphur dioxide which is released into the atmosphere and then combines with water to produce sulphuric acid which falls on trees, plants and fresh water life as acid rain. The effects from this are the destruction of plants, trees, fish and wildlife in much of Western Europe. The responsibility of the polluter should be taken far more seriously. There is a relationship between high levels of aluminium and the acidity of rainwater; the more acidic the rain the more potentially dangerous the water (see page 61).

Polluted rivers can contaminate our food supply through fish, irrigation of farming lands and reservoirs. It is encouraging to hear of once 'dead' rivers that now support salmon, trout and other freshwater life. Sadly, this change is very slow and there are still hundreds of miles of heavily polluted waterways.

Some of the possible contaminants found in water

- Aluminium

- Nitrates

- Chemical industrial waste

- Nuclear waste (in some areas only)

- Pesticide residues

- Heavy metals e.g., lead, cadmium, mercury

Man: the food chain connection

Man at the top of the food chain has the opportunity to eat a wide variety of foods rich in residues. The problem arises because many residues are soluble in fat, and thus stored in human body fat. Women naturally carry a larger amount of body fat than men. This means that they can potentially store more residues. Nature produces this extra fat store in readiness for pregnancy and lactation. Figures taken from *The Report of the Working Party on Pesticide Residues* (1982 to 1985) states that since 1976 pesticide residues in human beings have declined but not disappeared.

DDT in milligrams per kilo of fat			
1976 Average		**1982-3 Average**	
Male	Female	Male	Female
0.2	0.23	0.10	0.11

DDT has been officially banned as a pesticide for some years in Britain, but the figures state quite clearly that residues are still present in human body fat. Although no relationship has been drawn between these figures and ill health, we do not know the effect of long term slow release of residues from stored fat. Every day the body uses up a small amount of fat for energy which it replaces from daily food. Any residues in the body will therefore be released into the blood along with the fat as it is broken down. Those on slimming diets are likely to release more residues into their bloodstream.

An eminent farmer in the West Country has been looking at the effect of certain pesticide residues on cows. A group of cows was divided into those reared to Soil Association/Organic Standards and those reared on an agro-chemically based system. The farmer has found so far that those on an organic system have produced healthier calves, while several calves were born with abnormalities from those reared on an agro-chemically based system. These are teratogenic effects and may be similar in man. To counteract any possible teratogenic effects, it may be wise for women to change their diet to organically grown foods during pre-conception and pregnancy. For further details write to: Foresight, The Old Vicarage, Church Lane, Witley, Surrey GU8 5PN (Tel: (042879) 4500.

Having taken care to avoid contaminated food during pregnancy, it is prudent to continue to do so if breast-feeding. Breast milk has a fat content and therefore any potential residues in the mother's milk will be passed on to the baby. Modified cow's milk would not necessarily be any better in this respect because cows feed on treated grass land where the hazard still remains. MAFF has published figures on pesticide residues in human milk. Although since 1979 a general decline has been noted, residues are still present in breast milk.

DDT residues in breast milk

1979-1980 (milligrams/kilo)	1983-1984 (milligrams/kilo)
0.005	0.002

As mothers want the best for their children they will naturally want to minimize the risk of residues in their babies' diets. Breast milk is the very best food for all babies, and those who are concerned about the residue content of their breast milk should continue to breast-feed but change to an organic style of eating.

Feeding babies and young children

The nutritional needs of a child start even before he or she is born or even conceived. To give a child the best start in life it is wise to change your eating patterns for at least three months prior to conception. From scientific evidence and knowledge of such disease as Spina bifida we now know that foetal malformation can occur between day 19 and day 21 after the egg and sperm meet, before a woman is even aware that she is pregnant. Fuller details of the need for sound pre-conception nutrition are found in my book *The Twelve Month Pregnancy* which contains a complete nutritional guide for someone contemplating pregnancy. In addition to following these guidelines, a mother-to-be should wherever possible, eat only residue-reduced food and produce of organic origin. Foresight is a registered charity that provides advice about pre-conception care (address at the back of the book) and has a good selection of literature on this topic. It also helps researchers by providing some financial help in encouraging scientific research in this field. It also offers support to those with problems and a telephone advice service.

Babies and children need a balanced diet providing enough of all the essential nutrients. Guidelines on their nutritional needs are usually provided for new mothers through the hospital, National Child Birth Trust, pre-natal classes, health visitors, community midwives, doctors, paediatricians and nurses. Generally speaking, there should be ample opportunity available for every new mother to read up on the food requirements of their children.

Nevertheless, increases in dental problems, obesity, hyperactivity, other behavioural problems and intellectual impairment have been attributed to a junk food diet. There is a growing realization of the relationship between high fat diets and the deposition of arterial fats in a child from the time of birth until the child reaches the age of 10, which may be laying the foundation for later heart disease. We are now encouraged to reduce sugar, fats and salt in our diet and increase our fibre, fresh fruit, vegetables, white meat and fish intake, generally keeping to fresh foods, as opposed to a diet rich in convenience and junk foods.

These major changes have already started to happen, but not nearly as fast as they need to. Compared with children in other

European countries, British children are severely disadvantaged and when mothers are finally told and realize the truth they will vote with their purchasing power once again. Consumer power is the real way forward.

Baby foods

Feeding a baby should not be a difficult task. A great deal of information is available from reputable companies and through the health service. However, we should not become complacent. There have been incidents of baby food contamination. A certain baby food manufacturer famous for its rusks found a resilient bug in its production factory and lost millions of pounds worth of sales as a result.

Breast milk is quite rightly said to be the most perfect food for babies. However, the World Health Organization (WHO) is just beginning to bring to our attention the fact that toxic chemicals are being found in breast milk. A group of international experts believe that it is becoming such a problem that perhaps breast feeding should be completely abandoned – an example of the appalling side effects of exposure to toxic chemicals and their consequent accumulation in human body fat. The chemicals the WHO are concerned about are polychlorinated biphenyls (PCBs), polychlorinated dibenzo-p-dioxins (PCDDs) and polychlorinated dibenzofurans (PCDFs) as well as other chemical residues found in our food.

During the research for this report I spoke to Professor Donald Barltrop, consultant in child health at the Westminster Hospital, London. He said that he is surprised at the impact of the working party's findings (International Programme on Chemical Safety) but pleased that the issue is being taken seriously. He said that babies and young children must be considered a special case when considering the harmful effects of substances such as PCBs and other residues. As man is at the top of the food chain and has the most opportunities to become exposed to harmful chemicals, the concentrations of chemicals in human breast milk are of real concern.

Residues were also found in human breast milk by researchers, as described in the Report of the Working Party on Pesticide Residues by MAFF. During 1983 and 1984 samples of human breast milk were provided by mothers living in Scotland. These samples were analysed by researchers looking primarily at contamination from heavy metals, but also at residues of pesticides, polychlorobiphenyls and pentachloroanisole. From the results it appears that there are residues in human milk, but generally of a lower level than had been found in 1979. Nevertheless, these would be passed on to the baby through its mother's breast milk. The same report confirmed that residues were found in cow's milk, although it was not clear whether these residue amounts were on the decline or not.

Other reports have looked at the possible residue content of milk after cows had been either sprayed or dipped to get rid of the warble fly. Warble flies are one of several flies belonging to the Oestridae family, whose larvae form warbles inside the bodies of cattle, causing irritation and possible ill health.

Separate reports individually examined three different insecticides – Crufomate, Phosmet and Fenthion, to see for how long after treatment these three insecticides remained in the milk and to what extent. They confirmed that the insecticides found their way into the milk and remained there for up to two days afterwards. From examination of the milk it was generally noted that more of the insecticide accumulated in the cream, therefore any products made from the cream e.g., cheese, butter etc., would have an insecticide residue.

It was noted that skimmed milk had a lower content of insecticide residues. This could also correlate with findings amongst immunologists who find that those with a sensitivity to cow's milk can tolerate skimmed milk and not full cream milk.

Dipping is carried out intermittently on both cows and sheep, and because of this we shall all continually be receiving residues of insecticides in our milk and milk products. (And possibly in our meat too, although this is purely speculative.)

During research for this report we found a hypothesis concerning sudden infant death syndrome. At the time of going to press purely a *hypothesis* and in no way proven. The ideas expressed are at present purely speculative, but the figures and information supporting the hypothesis are accurate and genuine. The hypothesis is that: *contamination from the use of organophosphate insecticides or ingestion thereof may be at least a contributory cause of sudden infant death syndrome.*

The following facts support this hypothesis:

● Organophosphate insecticides are effective because they inactivate choline, an important micro-nutrient which contains certain enzymes which are needed for the uptake and metabolism of manganese. Manganese is an essential element involved in the mytochondria of cells and necessary for transporting oxygen in the blood to the brain.

● The use of organophosphates has peaked during the last decade. Figures for sudden infant death syndrome and for limb deformities have also risen during the same period. Although these could be said to bear no relationship, on the other hand perhaps they could.

Usage of organophosphates during 1971-1983

1971-1974		1975-1979		1980-1983	
Treated hectares	tonnes	Treated hectares	tonnes	Treated hectares	tonnes
845,800	430	975,000	534	923,000	591

London Food Commision Figures, June 1986

Sudden unexplained death 0-5 years	
1974	600
1975	634
1976	626
1977	690
1978	735

Limb deformities	
1974	4,338
1975	4,223
1976	4,227
1977	4,147
1978	4,157

Sudden infant death 0-2 years	
1979	874
1980	1,048
1981	1,085
1982	1,136
1983	1,133
1984	1,118

Limb deformities	
1979	5,491
1980	5,708
1981	5,305
1982	5,045
1983	5,245
1984	5,291

From the tables one can see that in 1979 the definition changed from sudden unexplained death 0-5 years to sudden infant death 0-2 years. We can therefore assume that any incidence of SID in 3-5 year olds and any limb deformities are not being recorded. If they were then the figures could be significantly higher.

● Mark Purdey, a farmer from Devon, moved farms. During this move some of his cows inadvertently ate some seed that had been treated with Thiram. The remaining cows in the herd did not eat any of the treated seed. From the first group (index herd) which ate the treated seed, four calves were born severely deformed with limb deformities, hydrocephalus, deformed spines and with a swelling of the basal brain stem. These calves were small and of the four, one died within hours of birth.

Other farmers have written to Mark Purdey regarding the use of organophosphates and have described similar deformities in calves. Mr Purdey charted these malformations on a geophysical map and found that the greatest numbers were occurring in farms where the soil was heavily limed. This can be antagonistic to manganese.

● From work carried out at Wayne State University, USA looking into manganese deficiency in breeding rats 'head retraction' was one of the abnormalities noted. This could be the result of brain stem abnormality.

● From work carried out at Guys Hospital, London it was revealed that babies who have an abnormal EEG (electro-encephalogram – a method by which electrical impulses derived from the brain can be amplified and recorded onto paper) are more at risk from sudden infant death. There also seems to be a link from this to walkers and sprayers who have been unfortunate enough to be overcome by organophosphate fumes and have had epileptic fits, in many cases for the very first time. Mark Purdey also revealed that one young farmer in the area suffered an epileptic seizure for the first time in his life after milking cattle dressed that morning with an organophosphorous warblecide.

Among the reported adverse reactions found in cattle after organophosphate dressings are muscle twitching; sweating; shivering; stilted movement; general weakness and ataxia of hind legs.

In more severe cases the animal tends to stagger. Inactivation of the body and limbs follow with the head being swung from side to side. Some attacks observed by Mr Purdey appeared to resemble epileptic fits in humans.

● SID babies are sometimes said to have respiratory disorders at the time prior to death. One of the reactions noted in observations of organophosphate treated animals is excessive nasal discharge and rapid breathing.

What might be learnt

Further research is desperately needed either to turn the hypothesis into hard fact or disprove it totally. Either way it could provide a very valuable contribution to the wealth of knowledge already collected on SID.

If you are planning a family and are worried about organo-phosphate contamination contact Foresight (address at the back of the book) for advice on the necessary steps to take. At the moment we do not have the necessary large scale analytical equipment here in Britain to routinely test for organophosphate residues in blood or breast milk. This is available only in the USA at Envirohealth Systems Inc., 990 North Bowser Road, Suite 880, Richardson, Texas 75081. This is not available through your own GP or the NHS, so you need either health insurance or to be able to pay privately for the treatment. For further details contact Dr Jean Munro's clinics (addresses and telephone numbers at the back of the book).

The baby food manufacturers

To find out more about the testing that is carried out on the raw materials used in the production of baby milks and baby foods we wrote to a number of manufacturers. We asked for their comments on their testing of these raw materials for antibiotics, growth promoters and pesticide residues, and the company's overall policy as to the acceptable levels of these residues in their products. Here are their replies:

The Boots Company plc

There is an obligation upon all food suppliers that the food should be fit for consumption and the suppliers of ingredients to us are as much covered by this obligation as we are to our customers.

As with food additives, the materials that can be used in association with foods for human consumption are controlled, both as to type and concentration, by government regulation. Thus the only pesticides and herbicides that are permitted to be used are specified, as also are the residues, if any, that may be left.

It is not practical to test all foodstuffs for possible infinitesimal traces of a multitude of complex chemicals, although where a particular chemical is suspected of being present in unusually large quantities (even though 'large' in this context may still only be expressed in parts-per-million) it is feasible to determine its presence.

We do not specify therefore a maximum level of these chemicals other than that the foodstuffs should conform to current legislation, but we do seek and expect that any such materials should be as low as possible and indeed, preferably absent. This is incorporated in the buying specification with suppliers.

Further to that, milk products are regularly tested for antibiotics (they are required to be absent) and raw materials and finished products for the baby foods are also regularly tested for pesticides, particularly organochlorine and organophosphorous residues.

H.J. Heinz Company Limited

At the moment, as you know, the UK appears to be moving towards statutory control of pesticide residues in foods. This would have the effect of bringing the UK into line with many EEC countries.

At H.J. Heinz we have always been conscious of food additives and contaminants. In the case of additives, we have always avoided their use where possible. This policy had originally been established by Henry Heinz, the founder of the company, in Pittsburgh, USA, at the beginning of the century in response to the widespread use of colour to disguise adulterated foods.

We use the facilities of the Food Research Association at Leatherhead for pesticide residue analysis of our ingredients, as well as at Harpenden where the Ministry work on pesticide safety is going on. We have very strict quality checks on all ingredients we use and only purchase raw materials from suppliers we know to be trustworthy in their farming practices.

We had heard through the National Childbirth Trust (NCT) that Heinz were about to restrict a number of pesticides used on crops for their baby foods. Unfortunately after asking them about this matter they replied:

'The action to withdraw approval for the use of 12 pesticides on baby food crops was in fact taken by our USA sister company and *not* Heinz UK. It coincided with a special review by the Environmental Protection Agency.'

Cow & Gate Limited said:

Cow & Gate Limited

The topics that you raise cover an extremely broad and complex spectrum. This makes it difficult for us to provide a detailed account of the precautions that we take to ensure that our products contain the minimum of these residues. However, we can assure you that we do have a detailed programme of monitoring which includes testing raw materials and finished products for a variety of items including: pesticides and herbicides, hormone growth promoters and antibiotics. In addition to this we do of course require that all of our raw materials and finished products conform to the latest EEC, DHSS, WHO and Codex standards.

We then phoned Cow & Gate to ask about their testing of raw materials and to generally discuss the issue of residues in raw materials. I spoke to their UK marketing director's secretary and before I could get back to speak to him personally I received a second letter:

'The Company position is as stated in my letter to you. I am afraid that I am not prepared to release any further information on this issue, so it really would be wasting your time to talk to me any further.'

Colman's of Norwich who manufacture Robinsons baby foods replied as follows:

Colman's

Thank you for your letter regarding the testing that we do of the raw materials that go into our baby foods. Obviously we test the materials on a routine basis for the obvious quality requirements and the acutely toxic materials that are controlled by legislation. It is not possible for us to equip ourselves for the measurement of the very small quantities of pesticides and other biologically active materials used in agriculture. We rely, in the main, on the warranties given to us by our suppliers plus the regular surveillance testing carried out by the MAFF and other bodies. As you will know the routine monitoring is carried out both on commodities as they are produced and on shopping basket surveys which relate more closely to food products as they are consumed. Recent reviews have shown that the number of samples found to contain levels of residues above the maximum recommended limits were approximately 1 per cent of the foods examined, while another review of pesticide residues presented a picture of generally low and declining levels although some occurrences did require attention.

Although we rely on our suppliers for the generally satisfactory state of our raw materials, we do occasionally arrange monitoring checks of our own and have not found any problems.

Wyeth Laboratories who manufacture the SMA baby milks wrote the following reply:

Wyeth Laboratories

I should like to assure the public that all raw materials used in the manufacture of our products are of the highest quality and as such are tested for antibiotics, growth promoters and pesticides.

From the letters and information received we have arrived at the following conclusions:

● There was a general reluctance on the part of the baby food producers who were contacted to give full details of their testing procedures.

● There was an absence of actual figures of residues found in raw materials.

● From the information received there was no evidence that these baby food manufacturers were looking towards residue-reduced baby products nor intending to offer organic quality baby foods in the near future as a choice for mothers.

Groups at risk

Babies and young children who are not eating an organic food diet and are not having filtered water are at greater risk than those who are eating organically grown foodstuffs although it is impossible to say how great the risk is. Babies who are being breast-fed by mothers who have been exposed to toxic chemicals at some time could be said to be at greater risk than those whose mothers have not been. This will be because the toxic residues will remain in the mother's body fat and could be re-metabolized and finding their way into breast milk.

Babies who are fed on modified cow's milk are also at risk because there always exists the possibility of exposure to chemical residues in the cow's milk. Cows have ample opportunities for exposure to a cocktail of different chemicals which we now know find their way into their milk. Young children on mixed feeding are at possible risk due to the chemical residues left behind in the raw materials that go into baby foods. The baby food manufacturers do test for residues but what levels do they consider? Any level of residual chemicals is unsatisfactory. Until we have fuller details it may be wise to switch to using Soil Association Standard organic foods and filter all the water that you give to your baby and yourself as a breast-feeding mother.

Practical pointers

● A growing number of manufacturers offer organic and partially organic quality baby foods.

Organic baby foods

Granose have told us that they test the raw ingredients of their baby foods for pesticide residues and growth promoters, including antibiotics in animal products. Their baby foods are vegetarian, organically grown, lactose free, contain no added colour, preservatives, sugar or salt and come in 190 gram sealed jars. Their range includes:

● **Vegetables with wholewheat noodles** contains vegetable purée (carrots, celery, fennel, potatoes), brown rice, almond cream, cold pressed sunflower oil, parsley.

● **Spring vegetables with 7 cereals** contains vegetable purée (carrots, potatoes, fennel), water, 7 cereals (wheat, rye, oats, barley, millet, spelt, brown rice), cold pressed sunflower oil, almond cream, parsley.

● **Spring vegetables with brown rice** contains vegetable purée (carrots, potatoes, fennel), water, brown rice, almond cream, cold pressed sunflower oil.

● **Carrots with apples** contains carrots, apples, water, honey, brown rice, acerola (cherries).

● **Mixed vegetables** – potatoes, carrots, water, celery, cold pressed sunflower oil, 7 cereals (wheat, rye, oats, barley, millet, spelt, rice), parsley, lemon juice.

● **Carrots and almond cream** – contains carrots, water, almond cream, brown rice, lemon juice.

● **Apple with pears and natural vitamin C** – contains apples, pears, honey, potatoes, brown rice, acerola (cherries), buckthorn.

● **7 Cereals with fruit** contains water, fruit purée (apples, peaches, raisins, dates), 7 cereals (wheat, rye, oats, barley, millet, spelt, brown rice), honey, almond cream, rosehip concentrate.

If you want further details write to Granose, Stanborough Park, Watford, Herts WD2 6JR (Tel: Watford (0923) 672281).

Bio-Familia AG, CH-6072 Sachsein, Switzerland produce the **Familia Swiss Baby Food.** All the raw ingredients used are grown organically (in Europe they call it organic-biological agriculture). It is a cereal-based breakfast product, with added nuts and apples.

Thursday Cottage produce a range of *organic* baby cereals (with the exception of those products containing soya flour as they have difficulty in obtaining adequate supplies of this flour). Their range includes rice, oats, barley, millet and a mixed cereal. For further details of retail outlets write to: Thursday Cottage Ltd., Spaxton, Bridgwater, Somerset TA5 1DD (Tel: 027867-330).

Several other organic baby products may be found in health food shops.

Drinks for babies and young children

Always choose organic juices if possible. There are a number of good ones in the food shops. One highly recommended juice is Copella apple juice because it is not made from imported concentrates as so many others are. Always avoid the 'junk juices' – those with additives and sugar. Boiled and cooled filtered water is always a preferable alternative. With children it is largely a question of training, so start early.

Organic baby milks

To-date we have not come across any organic baby milks but as concern over residues grows I am sure they will become available.

The way forward

If you are feeding a baby and are concerned about this issue do not become unduly alarmed. First consider adopting an organic food lifestyle and filtering your water. For those of you who are breast-feeding, eating organically grown foodstuffs and filtering your water will be the first steps towards protecting your baby from residues. Continuing to eat organic foods whilst you are breast-feeding will be a bonus and using organic baby foods will provide a healthier eating plan for your baby. Finally, when baby is seven or eight months old introducing some non-organic foods will hopefully not have any adverse effects. This particular age has been chosen as a baby's toleration level should be reasonably well established by then. If a food plan is based on these principles then babies are much less likely to develop allergic reactions and other health problems which could be attributed to exposure to certain chemicals.

CHAPTER 4

Organics in action
– *the farmer*

Does a farmer change from an agro-chemically based farm to an organic farm for economic or philosophical reasons? Often it will be because he has felt ill at ease with the 'intensive' approach to the land. Many farmers are now picking up the threads of the harmony they used to have with the land.

The labour-saving chemicals on offer to the farmer have often been too much to resist. How much quicker and easier it is to remove unwanted weeds by spraying with a herbicide using physical and mechanical methods. But consider the knock-on effect this single action can have on the animals and plants living in a field. Firstly the insects that depend on those weeds for their food will now have gone. So the birds who eat these will be affected in two ways – by eating contaminated insects and by their food source becoming depleted. This is only part of the problem of how the food chain plays an important part in our long-term good health (see page 91).

Certain modern intensive livestock farming techniques result in over-crowding of livestock. They are deprived of hours in the air and sunshine and the freedom to roam. There is an excessive use of medication to combat cross-infection and environmental stress. The feeding regimes used in intensive farming are geared to quick results i.e., feed additives, growth promoters, use of highly concentrated feeds, leading to an imbalance in supply and demand and resulting in the ever-increasing, embarrassing stockpiling of foodstuffs.

Lawrence Woodward, in a paper entitled 'The Alternative View' in *Organic Farming* (May 1984), summarizes the reasons farmers have for wanting to farm organically.

'The motivation for farmers to turn to organic methods is very similar in the USA, Britain and the rest of Europe. Soil health, good husbandry and stewardship of the land, concern for human and animal health, the fear of agro-chemicals, the desire to improve food quality and an active concern for the environment being the major reasons.' (Taken from *The future for organically grown produce* by Claude E. Hill, 1986).

Using organic methods would redress the balance of supply meeting demand, and a modest surplus could also be achieved. It would put people back into long term employment because of the resulting need for extra manpower in organic agriculture.

At first glance, organic farming looks more expensive for the farmer. However, although the agro-chemical farmer may end up with a greater quantity of produce to sell in a shorter space of time, the inputs into agro-chemically based farms are many times greater: specialized equipment, the ever-increasing cost of fertilizers, pesticides, antibiotics, feed additives, etc. There is no doubt that some farmers have started to farm organically because of lower capital requirements, lower interest repayments and lower risks. A study carried out at University College, Aberystwyth in 1981 found that 28 per cent of organic farmers quoted such reasons.

Initially organic foods (residue-free) may be more expensive but as methods are streamlined, reduced costs to the consumer will result. It is only through investment by the consumer that organic foods will take a significant share of the food market. As yet the marketing or organic food is limited. It could provide a golden opportunity for an enterprising marketing company to take the whole concept of organics and give it a modern, sellable image. The opportunities are limitless. A whole new food industry could be built around the organic image.

What's in it for the consumer:
● The opportunity to choose residue-free produce.

● With the uncertainty of the health hazards associated with long term low level exposure to chemical residues in food, it makes sense to avoid them whenever possible.

● The consumer who buys organic produce has peace of mind in the knowledge that she is not putting herself or her family at unnecessary risk.

• Better flavoured fruit and vegetables with more nutrients per ounce because of a lower water content.

• A farmer who is concerned about the health of his customers is more likely to insist on selling quality produce.

The Boxworth Field Station Project

To find out the real effect of pesticides on the lives of insects and small mammals, the Boxworth Field Station in Cambridgeshire has been monitoring these effects. Three different plots of land (all fertilized) are being looked at for:

• Excessive pesticide use.

• Recommended amount used.

• No pesticides at all.

The results of this study will be published at a later date.

The Soil Association

The Soil Association was founded as a charity in 1946, long before the present consumer interest in healthy eating. It was created to further the philosophy of interrelated wholeness. The Association encourages an ecological approach to agriculture and offers organic husbandry as the long term alternative to intensive techniques. Through information and education it hopes to bring together and increase the numbers of those who believe in a healthy, safe and sustainable approach to food production and nutrition.

The Soil Association is not a commercial operation, but acts as a body which sets standards for organic production.

The Soil Association Standards for Organic Produce – Conforming to the standard drawn up by the British Organic Standards Committee 1983

Conversion
Produce may generally only be sold under the SA symbol after a conversion period of the land of at least two years after a satisfactory

plan has been agreed with the SA inspectorate. During the conversion period new techniques and good husbandry management are learnt. Once this cleansing period is over, true organic farming can begin. As a result of over-use of agro-chemicals some land may take up to 20 years to be free from agro-chemical residues, so it should be emphasized that a personal plan is needed for every individual farmer. After the conversion period every farmer must keep to the SA specified methods of organic farming. Only if these methods are followed correctly will a farmer be able to label his produce as 'organic' with the SA symbol.

Soil Association Standards are divided into three general areas:

- general husbandry,

- livestock husbandry and

- final product

General husbandry standards

- ### Manures and compost manures
Manure from all types of livestock on the farm should be used, preferably composted with straw and/or other crop by-products. Any bought-in manures must be approved by the SA inspectorate. The SA recognizes that suitable organic matter may be available from agro-chemically based farms, providing the level of toxic residues and heavy metals are within the SA permitted range. If above SA levels the inspectorate may insist on the treatment of these manures before use. It must be noted that the SA does not approve of the methods on the agro-chemically based farm to produce these manures.

Animal slurry should be used with discretion, as over-use is harmful to worms. Sewage sludge may be used, but not more than once in every three years after the appropriate soil tests.

- ### Animal by-products
Shoddy (waste from the woollen industry) often contains persistent toxic residues caused by sheep dipping. Therefore the use of shoddy is not allowed. Dried blood is a good source of nitrogen and can be used with care up to a maximum of three cwts per acre. Any

other animal by-products should be checked with the SA inspectorate.

● **Vegetable by-products**

Vegetable by-products e.g., spent hops, apple waste and straw (which can contain residues of agro-chemical treatments) are only allowed on approval of the SA. Sawdust, woodshaving and bark can be used if they come from timber not chemically treated.

● **Mineral fertilizers**

The following fertilizers are allowed: basic slag, ground phosphate rock, dolomite (magnesium limestone), felspar, adularian shale (rock potash), gypsum (calcium sulphate), ground chalk.

● **Seaweed products**

The use of fresh seaweed, ground calcareous seaweed, seaweed meal and pure seaweed foliar feeds are allowed.

● **Insect control**

The following products are allowed: pure pyrethrum, derris (dangerous to fish and should not be used near water courses), garlic, herbal and homoeopathic preparations and quassia.

● **Biological pest control**

The following organisms are permitted:

Encarsia formosa; phystosieulus persimilis; bacillus thuringiensis; trichodema viride and Cephalosporium lecanii.

This list is continually being added to and should therefore be checked.

● **Fungus control**

The following fungicides are allowed on plants: potassium permanganate, sodium silicate (water glass), herbal and homoeopathic sprays and preparations. Dispersible sulphur and copper fungicides are also allowed. Only steam soil sterilization is permitted.

● **Herbicides**

No herbicides are allowed under any circumstances.

● **Miscellaneous**

Growth inhibitors or a combination of growth regulators and inhibitors, like those used on standing corn are forbidden. Sprout inhibitors for potatoes are not allowed. Dressed seed, in particular mercurial seed dressings, should be avoided. New products should be approved by the inspectorate before use.

If any breakdown of the system occurs necessitating the use of any prohibited materials the inspectorate must be notified and the field/fields in question will have to revert to being considered as in conversion. The inspectorate will deal with each case on its own merit.

Livestock husbandry standard

Animal rearing should be based on ethical consideration, animal needs and patterns that have evolved over millions of years.

The European Convention on Farm Animals requires that they should be kept according to their physiological and ethological needs. This would rule out cages, tethering and penning except for short periods, unsuitable feeding, growth promoters or other interference with the normal growth pattern.

The SA says its methods are as economically viable, and in some cases more so, than today's practices.

● Housing of livestock

The accommodation should allow free movement of stock, and a sleeping area with adequate bedding. The building should allow the maximum amount of fresh air and daylight, and adequate regular access to pasture for all the animals during fair weather. Permanent housing of breeding stock is prohibited.

● Management practices

Growth hormone injections and vaccinations to remove natural growth controls are prohibited.

The detailing and removal of teeth in pigs is prohibited, except for veterinary reasons due to accident or disease.

● Feeding

All grazing land must have herbage grown to Soil Association standard. Every effort should be made to provide feed produced to SA's general husbandry standard. Where this becomes impossible there is some leeway, allowing up to 20 per cent of the dry matter of the daily intake to be from non-organic origin.

Food supplemented with growth promoters (including copper for pigs), antibiotics and hormones is prohibited.

The following mineral additives are allowed; rock salt, calcified seaweed, seaweed powder and steamed bone flour for deficiencies due to actual mineral deficiency in the soil on a short-term basis, but only in consultation with the inspectorate. The use of any other mineral additive without inspectorate clearance is prohibited.

Added vitamins are only permissible when they are known to have come from a natural source e.g., cod liver oil and yeast. The use of urea is prohibited. It is also desirable to avoid the use of synthetic amino acids, antioxidants, emulsifiers and chemical colourants that may influence the colour of egg yolks (tartrazine). The use of feed containing animal manure is also prohibited. The use of coccidiostats and anti-blackhead drugs in the early stages of poultry rearing is tolerated, but only until further research provides the SA with a viable alternative.

For use in veterinary medicine, herbal and homoeopathic remedies are strongly advised. However, the SA realizes that much research and development has to take place to produce effective and viable products and until there are satisfactory alternatives the following are permitted in the case of an emergency: antibiotics and other drugs, anthelmintics for fluke, lung and gutworm infestation, and livestock vaccines. However, the use of such products should be declared to the inspectorate.

Routine use of other drugs and antibiotics are not allowed, including intermammary application of antibiotics for dairy cows. The use of organophosphorus compounds for warble fly disqualifies the producer from using the symbol for meat and milk products for a period to be decided at the discretion of the inspectorate.

Final product standards	
Products	**Comment**
Meat	Only from animals and poultry reared to SA's general and livestock husbandry standard
Liquid milk and cream	Only from animals kept to SA's general livestock husbandry standard
Butter	Only from milk produced to SA's general livestock husbandry standard. Sea salt must be used. Chemical colourants are not permitted. Aluminium containers and equipment for any milk product are not recommended.

Final product standards

Products	Comment
Cheese	Only from milk produced to SA's general livestock husbandry standard. Only sea salt should be used. Only herbs grown to SA's standard, natural spices and aromatic plants may be used. Colourants and chemical additives are prohibited. Equipment must not be greased with liquid paraffin.
Plain yogurt	Only from milk produced to SA's livestock and general husbandry standard. All other additives other than bacterial starter are prohibited.
Fruit yogurt	Fresh or preserved fruit can be used but must be grown to SA's standard.
Eggs	Only from hens kept in accordance with the SA's livestock and general husbandry standard.
Vegetables and fruit	Must be grown to SA's general husbandry standard. Post-harvest chemical treatment is prohibited.
Fruit juices	Must be from fresh fruit grown to SA's general husbandry standard. Colourants, sulphur dioxide, antioxidants, preservatives and artificial flavours are prohibited.
Cider	Only from fresh apples grown to SA's standard. Colourants, dried or pulped apples treated with sulphur dioxide, antioxidants, preservatives and artificial flavourings are prohibited.
Cider vinegar	As above. Fermentation must be by natural processes, the use of acetic acid is prohibited.
Jams	Only from fresh fruit grown according to SA's standard. Natural beet syrup and unrefined sugars are preferred. It is recommended that non-stick or aluminium cookware is avoided. Colourants, antioxidants, preservatives, artificial flavourings are prohibited.
Cereals and cereal products	Whole grains, grain flakes and flour must be from cereals grown according to the SA's general husbandry standard. Flour used in

---

Final product standards

Products	Comment
	bread making should be of SA's standard. Other ingredients including yeast, natural leaven, sea or rock salt, biosalt, vegetable oil (cold pressed) honey or approved molasses, milk, soya milk should be used.
	Artificial leavening processes, mineral oils e.g., liquid paraffin and preservatives are prohibited.
	Chemical treatments for storage are prohibited.
	Non-stick and aluminium cookware should be avoided. Tin-greasing oil should be cold-pressed vegetable oil

---

• In conclusion

The Soil Association does feel that these standards have some shortcomings. However, with increased knowledge and development of techniques, production can rapidly be improved and continue to develop. For detailed guidelines write to: The Soil Association, 86-88 Colston Street, Bristol BS1 5BB (Tel: 0272 290661).

Farm Verified Organic

The marketing agency Farm Verified Organic matches up organic producers with consumers. The Government has never given a clear definition of the term 'organically grown'; as a result, consumers have been confused, and organic foods have not been able to take a representative share of the market.

The informed consumer will now be able to obtain full and detailed guarantees. Farm Verified Organic is an internationally-accepted verification programme for organic food, backed by an independent system of inspection. It is in operation in the United States, Europe and now in Britain. FVO uses clear organic standards, making it easy for farmer, manufacturer and consumer to recognize acceptable products. All food stuffs that come from a member are of the organizations standards. The Soil Association is the standard setting body (see page 118) but as products pass through many different hands, traders, manufacturers, processors etc., FVO integrates all these stages by a stringent system of checks and records.

What is unique is that a product specification sheet describes how products are grown, and a signed affidavit from the actual producer is a written assurance that the product complies with FVO standards. FVO uses a lot number system to trace products from farm to consumer. Members are visited regularly to discuss practical matters such as approved suppliers and correct labelling of products.

To give credibility FVO has appointed an independent evaluation panel taken from a cross section of the food industry and asked them to report on the entire operation.

To the consumer who has never bought organic produce, this is the best system. It takes away any possible doubt as to food origin. This is obviously a major step forward for those who want a residue-free diet.

Among companies belonging to FVO are:

Living Foods,
P.O. Box 66, Chichester PO18 9HH

The Lincolnshire Wine Company,
Ludborough, Near Grimsby DN36 5SJ

The Organic Wine Company Ltd.,
P.O. Box 81, High Wycombe, Bucks HP11 1LJ

Springhill Farm Foods Ltd.,
Mouse Lane, Steyning, W. Sussex BN4 3DF

A new organic fresh loaf is being launched as a result of collaboration between Springhill Bakers and Sarah Franklyn of Fernham Bakery. Although this will probably be only available locally it is a positive step in the right direction. Coffee also is being added to the FVO list. There are over 100 products on this list and as trends change the number will grow to meet demands. For further details of Farm Verified Organic write to: Tony Mason, 86 Easton Street, High Wycombe, Bucks HP11 1LT (Tel: 0494 459922; Telex: 83686).

Organic Farmers and Growers Limited

David Stickland, one of the directors of Organic Farmers and Growers describes this farmers' co-operative which has 169 member farms.

● 'I have been hooked on organic farming since 1949, and the reason I got very keen on it was that I like the way of dairy farming organically rather than using the chemicals that were then in general use. I was not too concerned about human beings then because they have a choice and cows do not. Having been in agriculture ever since a child, but not always organic, I have always had an interest in it and ended up with my own organic farm in New Zealand. The really simple answer of why I do it is because I like it. It is a nice way of farming: I do not like a lot of the chemicals that are used.

● As the soil improves, the life in the soil improves, and so the crops are healthier, the farming itself is pleasant because chemicals are not involved, it is a method of farming which can go for ever without the worry of not being able to get supplies because of oil shortages and strikes. I like the way that the fertilizers we use work in the soil rather than being water soluble and on the whole it is farming as near to Nature's method of growing crops as one can get. Bearing in mind there is nothing natural about farming in any case, and that Nature has evolved a system over millions of years which works very well, working as near to that system as possible is the best way. I have achieved these aims by experience over many years, and a lot of reading and hard work.

● We are the largest producers of organic grain for the health food market, we have farmers contacting us all the time now, we are approached by all sorts of people in the agricultural movement, and in general our farming has gone from being 'cranky' and ignored until two or three years ago it became respectable and is now potentially the largest growth area in agriculture.

● We have farmers now producing gross margins higher than any other crops on their farm, and we have farmers up to 4,000 acres. If the farm is managed well the system is very viable because of the premiums and because of the low cost. If the farm is not managed well it is no better than any chemical method.

● As far as we are concerned we cannot keep up with demand and never have been able to in the 12 years of OF & G's existence. Now we have the very big companies coming to us who have shunned us for years. The future is very good if we can get the crops grown, and as more conventional farmers are coming to us than ever before this is gradually beginning to look possible. We are now into vegetables with the supermarkets, and in general, if anything we are too busy. So the future, for the next ten years at least, has to be good, provided that we can get the crops and provided that the government or the EEC do not intervene and bring in rules that have standards far too tight and narrow for anyone to follow. This has already happened in some European countries.

● I do not have facts and figures to support our methods from the point of view of organic foods being healthier, but we do have plenty of people who come to us who have allergies if they eat chemically treated foods. We are not imagining it, because quite often they do not know they are eating food with chemicals. Then their allergies come back. But we have plenty of others who say they feel healthier eating organic food, that they can taste it better and so on.'

For further details write to: Organic Farmers and Growers Limited,

Abacus House, Station Yard, Needham Market, Ipswich, Suffolk IP6 8AT (Tel: 0449 720838; Telex Chamcom Ipswich 987703).

Guild of Conservation Food Producers

This organization has set a standard of its own in the growing, processing and marketing of certain foods. The Guild produces foods by avoiding reliance on potentially harmful food additives and treatments of soil, plants and animals. The Guild aims to produce foods free of toxic chemicals, while still maintaining adequate and substantial yields. It operates an inspection system and promotes farming methods that are beneficial to our eco system.

All food grown by Guild members will be clearly labelled with the Conservation Grade Symbol. The consumer will know that these foods have been produced using limited intervention and are substantially residue-reduced but not organic. Food processors too will also have to adhere to the Guild's monitoring system.

A significant fact about the Guild is that it rightly associates allergic reactions with residues in our food, whether they be pesticide, additive or hormone in origin.

Guild of Conservation Food Producers, PO Box 157, Bedford Way MK42 9BY (Tel: Bedford (0234) 61626).

Training in organic methods

There is no government-funded organic agricultural college. Anyone interested must be prepared to finance his or her own education. **The Bio-Farming Register** run by Country College, 10 Hamilton Road, Alford, Lincs LN13 9HD (Tel: Alford (052 12) 6348) can provide a classified list of lecturers and teachers expert in their particular field. Little exists in the way of residential full time courses. **Emerson College,** Pixton, Forest Row, Sussex RH18 5JX (Tel: Forest Row (034 282) 2238) offers full time courses of one to three years in bio-dynamic farming and the Horticultural Training College, Arkley Manor Farm, Rowley Lane, Arkley, near Barnet, Herts EN3 3HS (Tel: 01-449 7944) runs one year full time, non residential courses. There are also smaller bodies, such as the Yarner Trust, Welcome Barton, Welcombe, Bideford, North Devon (Tel: Morwenstow (028 883) 482) which offers experience of small scale organic farming, smallholding and self reliant community life. Students practise crop and livestock production methods, domestic skills (cheese, butter, breadmaking, food preservation and other rural skills e.g., carpentry, coppicing, building).

For those with limited time or funds the best solution may be a combination of the Country College practical correspondence course 'Organic Crop Production' and the various facilities offered by WWOOF (Working Weekends on Organic Farms) which provide the opportunity to experience organic farming and growing at a practical level on a variety of farms, small holdings and gardens throughout the UK for any mutually convenient length of time. More formally, the WWOOF Training Scheme (WTS) is a flexible, self help apprenticeship scheme which links serious students with a network of commercial and non-commercial enthusiasts prepared to teach specific skills. A directory of organizations and training opportunities in the UK organic movement can be obtained from WWOOF, 19 Bradford Road, Lewes, E. Sussex BN7 1RB.

National Federation of City Farms

This is an autonomous community enterprise that encourages organic and sustainable farming with an ecological approach to the conservation and management of land and resources. It actively promotes the involvement of all people in the locality in a wide range of social and economic activities that meet the needs of the community; in particular through farming activities. Farming is conducted in a framework of good animal husbandry and welfare practices together with sound ecological, horticulture, arboriculture and cropping methods. It provides children and adults, the able-bodied and the handicapped with a chance to experience rural activities in their own neighbourhood every day. It provides a basis for understanding the local environment as well as introducing the countryside beyond and an opportunity for improving the local environment. For further information and addresses of farms and gardens write to: The Old Vicarage, 66 Fraser Street, Windmill Hill, Bedminster, Bristol BS3 4LY (Tel: (0272) 660663).

The Permaculture Association

This is a registered charity which aims to encourage the practice of permaculture – a design system for sustainable agriculture, horticulture and forestry. Many techniques are used e.g., organic growing and pest control techniques, old forestry practices such as coppicing; technology for energy conservation and the use of solar energy and recycling of wastes. All the different elements are consciously designed to work together to produce a varied yield, so that failure of one crop is a minor setback, not a major disaster. Each element in the system – plants, animals, buildings, water, landscape features should have more than one function. For example, chickens are most efficient (and happiest) when able to behave naturally – scratch, forage, make manure, lay eggs. They can be used to clear and manure ground, eat weeds and orchard pests, provide night heat in a glasshouse, as well as providing eggs, feathers and meat.

The basic practical aims of a permaculture design are:

● Emphasis on perennial rather than annual crops, especially trees.

● Combination of diverse activities: gardening, farming, poultry, acquaculture, tree and shrub planting etc.

● Recycling of all materials.

● High species diversity, often with close planting.

● Use of three-dimensional space – trees, shrubs, vines and low growing plants using different levels of soil and light, and increasing total yield.

● Minimum tillage.

● Use of small scale machinery and hand tools.

● Layout minimizing walking and transportation.

● Close relationship between land usage and climatic features and the location and design of buildings and their uses.

Permaculture is applicable to urban as well as rural situations and can be practised on any scale: balcony or roof, glasshouse, garden, farm or estate.

Further information from 8 Hunters Moon, Dartington, Totnes, Devon TQ9 6JT (Tel: 0803 865115).

The Institute for Social Inventions

The Institute for Social Inventions at 24 Abercorn Place, London NW8 9XP (Tel: 01-229 7253) offers £1,000 in prizes each year for the best social inventions proposed by members of the public, adult or children with an annual deadline of June 1. A social invention is a new and imaginative solution to a social problem and one that improves the quality of life. Good examples include Live Aid, the Open University, Community Service Volunteers and Voluntary Service Overseas. The Institute is a non profit making association launched in 1985 with the aim of promoting social inventions. It brings together experienced 'project makers' who provide an informal experiences social enterprise agency for others trying to launch projects.

CHAPTER 5

Organics in action
– *the consumer*

Wine today has become so varied that we now have specialists who spend their entire time considering the worth of countless bottles; many today consider themselves 'wine buffs'. Indeed the agrochemical industry has been so successful in ensuring large, luscious harvests that the ordinary man's desire to acquire this taste of luxury has been fulfilled.

Wine and the consumer

Wine has become so popular that average consumption in Britain over the past 10 years has gone from 9.4 pints to 17 pints per year. In response to this demand for wine, some vineyards have had to make use of sophisticated technology. As they have moved away from traditional methods they have had to employ the services of chemists to help produce 'constantly' acceptable products in the quantity that British supermarkets demand.

Since the Austrian and German wine scandals where wine was knowingly contaminated with a potential poison diethylene glycol (anti-freeze) the consumer has come to realize that today's wine is not a truly natural product. As a result of the deaths from drinking this contaminated wine the consumer demands safeguards against the likelihood of this happening again. Austrian wine exports have fallen to a drastically low level.

A large number of different additives can be used in wine production. Here is the list of permitted wine additives available for use in wine production (taken from EEC Regulation 337 – 1979 HMSO).

Additives

● **Yeasts** - cultured to control fermentation.

● **Diammoniumphosphate, ammonium sulphate, thiamin hydrochloride** used for feeding yeast.

● **Sulphur dioxide, potassium disulphate, potassium metabisulphate** - the wine-maker's antiseptic. These stop bacteria spoilage slowing down the yeast and prevent oxidation.

● **Sorbic acid, potassium disulphate** to slow down the action of yeast.

● **Potassium tartrate, potassium bicarbonate, calcium carbonate** for de-acidification of English and German wines. **Potassium** is allowed in all EEC countries.

● **Carbon dioxide** - used in cheaper, sparkling wine.

● **Citric acid** - an acidity regulator.

● **Tannin** - to help give extra body, and provide a full flavour.

● **Potassium ferrocyanide** - used to colour red wines.

● **Metartartic acid, malic acid, potassium, tartaric acid** - used to precipitate calcium. Produces the naturally occurring white crystals.

● **Sugar** - a poor summer results in grapes having very little natural sugar (fructose). Sucrose is then used as a supplement. This practice is now being phased out and concentrated crushed grapes (musts) are being used.

● **Copper sulphate** - silver chloride, sodium-based cations (positively charged ions) to reduce sulphide levels.

● **Calcium carbonate, potassium bicarbonate, neutral potassium tartrate** - used as de-acidifying agents.

Treatments for clearing wines

● Edible gelatine

● Isinglass

- Casien and potassium caseinate
- Egg white
- Dried blood powder (animal albumins)
- Bentonite clay
- Sturgeon's air bladders
- Silicon dioxide
- Kaolin
- Charcoal
- Pectinolytic enzymes
- Potassium kaolinite

The making of wine

The traditional method of making wine is to crush the grapes, allowing the yeasts on the grape skin to come into contact with the natural sugars present and allowing them to ferment into alcohol and carbon dioxide. When the alcohol content reaches 15 per cent the fermentation stops naturally and a dry wine is produced.

To speed up the production of wine, viticulturists can use a selection of permitted additives and techniques to control the process. This ensures consistent results and quantity.

Sadly this technique has become almost too successful and in the EEC there is generally an excess of wine commonly known as the 'wine lake'. To reverse this situation an EEC Action Programme on Wine (1980-1985) prohibited the use of sugar which was replaced by extra grape juice, thereby reducing the overall quantity of wine produced.

During an examination of additives used in wine making, sugar was the only one to receive real attention. There was no decision to consider the other additives. If there were to be a change in the labelling policy of wine production i.e., compulsory identification of all contents as we have seen elsewhere in the food industry the consumer would be able to make a more informed choice. Some wine producers have fought against any introduction of labelling. They insist that it would be expensive and that accuracy would be difficult. The consumer does now however have a choice of a selection of organic wines where the history of origin is quite clear. One of the companies concerned also belongs to the Farm Verified Organic, an extra guarantee to the consumer.

Here is a list of organic wine suppliers and background details.

Vintage Roots

This company is run by an interesting trio. They wanted to start up a viable business with a flavour of the alternative about it and since one of them – Pete – is half French and fluent in the language, they took the plunge with some of their own money and the help of the Government's Enterprise Allowance Scheme.

They bought a van and went to France to buy their wine direct. This is good news for British consumers as they will be guaranteed a true organic product. Vintage Roots feel that by direct contact with individual vineyards they will establish good relationships with the growers. They are making great efforts to contact the growing number of organic wine growers and now know of over 100 in France, Germany and Italy. They are confident that demand will grow for two main reasons:

● Consumers are now aware of the additive and possible pesticide residue content of wine and prefer as natural a product as possible.

● The quality wines sold have a character all their own. Vintage Roots, 88 Radstock Road, Reading, Berks RG1 3PR (Tel: 0734 662659).

West Heath Wines

Their catalogue emphasizes the fact that their organic wines are made from grapes that have not been sprayed with synthetic chemical pesticides, herbicides or fungicides. They are produced by independent growers using traditional biodynamic methods.

To ensure high yields and average quality the majority of growers are heavily dependent on chemicals. Vines can be sprayed as many as 14 times each year with sprays that are possibly arsenic and nicotine-based pesticides (see pesticide list).

West Heath Wines are concerned about the long term effects of these methods, not only on human health but on the environment too. They are active proponents of equivalent legislation in the drinks industry as exists already in the food industry. They provide a wide selection of reasonably priced wines.

West Heath, Pirbright, Surrey GU24 0QE (Tel: 048 67 6464).

The Lincolnshire Wine Company

Konrad Knodel gives a very full and interesting account of how he became a purveyor of organic wines. Here is part of the letter he sends to his customers explaining his methods of wine making:

'I changed production from the vineyards of my great-grandfather to organic methods in 1977 and from then onwards we no longer used any mineral salts or chemical fertilizers. The pursuit of intensive ground treatment and compost economy using castor oil plant meal, bonemeal, tree bark, straw, stoneflour (mineral), compost of pressed grapeskins and organic materials falling in the vineyards such as vine branches, leaves, twigs etc., ensured a lush and varied flora and fauna on our fields . . . For over six years no insecticides have been sprayed.

To fight fungal disease we do not use the chemical methods that are customary, but elementary materials and strong preparations made of herbs and stoneflour. The grapes are hand-picked, pressed and the cultivation of the must follows, in wooden barrels. When the wine has fermented in the spring the new wine is carefully drawn off.'

The Lincolnshire Wine Company, Chapel Lane, Ludborough, Nr. Grimsby (Tel: 0472 87858).

The Organic Wine Company Ltd

The introduction to their catalogue reads: 'At its simplest, organically produced wine means using the most natural ingredients possible', information certainly attractive to the consumer constantly on the look-out for residue free products.

It continues: 'Modern wine-making techniques have tended to produce wines which are strictly controlled at every stage of their production. In many cases, vines are planted for their yield rather than the character of the crop.' The Organic Wine Company is obviously very strict in its adherence to organic principles, almost to the pitch of crusading fervour. It also makes one very important point that all consumers should bear in mind: all wines use sulphur dioxide for stability but organic wines use the very minimum.

The Organic Wine Company, P.O. Box 81, High Wycombe, Bucks HP11 1LJ (Tel: 0494 446557).

To those who have an allergy (intolerance) to sulphur dioxide it can under certain circumstances cause very unpleasant symptoms. In some cases people have had to be hospitalized. How do you know if you are sensitive to sulphur dioxide?

Symptoms of sulphur dioxide sensitivity*

- Flashing lights and blurred vision.
- Irregular breathing and breathlessness. In some cases asthma attacks have been brought on.
- Nervous irritability.

It would be difficult to provide a full list as allergies (intolerance levels) are different in each person.

There is one experiment you could try: drink a bottle of regular supermarket wine one day and then a bottle of organic wine the next day. Note the results. Perhaps you've been suffering hangovers needlessly for years!

After an impromptu wine tasting session with eight participants, the overall feeling was that the best organic wines were excellent, but others did not compare to some supermarket wines. However, the group felt 'real wine' would become popular as people were becoming concerned by the amount of contaminants they were

* For further details of sulphur dioxide sensitivity read: *Chemical Children* by Dr Jean Monro and Dr Peter Mansfield (Century Paperbacks). Although a book describing problems suffered by children, there is a great deal of useful information in it for adults.

consuming. As the wine gains popularity the variety and quality will develop.

The wine tasters said they would like the opportunity to buy organic wine in their local supermarket. They would like to be able to try each new year's wine and would accept that some years' crop might be awful. This would make the drinking of wine more interesting; the group felt a certain amount of boredom had crept into wine drinking lately and that the arrival of organic wine could rekindle interest.

These are a set of labels from organic wine bottles, the very bottom of the label is the most interesting as these symbols denote organic quality. A symbol to look out for if you want wine without pesticides or herbicides.

Beer and the consumer

Over 30 million pints of beer are drunk in Britain almost every day. It would be safe to say that if there were any possible adverse effects from residues they would show themselves in a very short space of time.

The labelling of beer containers is not yet compulsory. There are, however, a small number of independent brewers who are concerned about the quality of raw ingredients and are actively encouraging the consumer to read the list of ingredients. These are very basic and exclude any chemical additives.

Additives that may be found in beer

There are no laws governing the composition of beer and so the substances on the following list are in no way illegal. Many are 'adjuncts', meaning that they are used during processing and are not necessarily present in the final product.

Preservatives

The Preservatives in Food regulations have put a limit of 70 mg/kg in beer of the following additives:

- Sulphur dioxide

- Benzoic acid

- Methyl 4-hydroxybenzoate or ethyl 4-hydroxybenzoate or Propyl 4-hydroxybenzoate.

Clarifying agents and fining agents

The heavy use of fertilizers has produced barley with a high nitrogen content. This gives brewers problems, not only because of the possibility of nitrosamines (see nitrates, page 72, for explanation) being produced but also because it makes the beer cloudy. Additives are used to clear the beer by encouraging the formation of solids that take these substances to the bottom of the tanks for them to be removed. The additives used are:

- Sodium alginate

- Carrageen and carrageenan

- Furcellaran

- Agar and gum arabic (acacia)

- Isinglass

- Silica solution

- Cellulose powder

- Silica hydrogel

- Tannin

Beer can also be filtered through asbestos sheets. The Food Standards Committee allows this because toxicity committees have found no evidence of health risks from levels of asbestos in beer but it added 'every effort should be made by the brewing industry to find a suitable alternative'.

Beer head control agents

Certain yeasts are responsible for the formation of a head on beer and additives may be used to control yeast-head formation. One such substance is Dimethylpolysiloxane. Vitamins and minerals can also be added to improve the yeast's performance.

It is also assumed that the consumer expects the head on his beer to last and therefore propane-1-2-diolalginate is allowed, subject to the toxicity committee receiving satisfactory safety tests on this stabilizing beer foam additive.

'Burtonizing' agents

Since beer is basically water, the quality of the water has a great influence on the end product. In Britain brewers often try to give beer a 'Burton' character by altering the composition of their water to mimic that used in breweries in the Burton upon Trent area. The following are used to achieve this effect:

- Acetic acid
- Calcium chloride
- Orthophosphoric acid
- Potassium bisulphate
- Calcium hydroxide
- Calcium sulphate
- Hydrochloric acid
- Magnesium sulphate
- Potassium chloride
- Sodium hydroxide
- Sodium sulphate
- Sulphuric acid

Agents to reduce carbohydrate loss and protein breakdown
The following additives are used during the malting process:

- Potassium bromate

- Sodium bromate

- Sulphur dioxide

- Sulphuric acid

- Phosphoric acid

- Hydrochloric acid

- Citric acid

- Acetic acid

- Lactic acid

Germination agents
Gibberellic acid is allowed to be used as a supplement to natural hormones in germinating barleys. (Gibberellens are also sprayed on grapes to encourage large fruit. You may have noticed recently that the shape of the average grape has changed; this is due to adding extra gibberellens to those naturally present.)

Pesticides
The Food Standards Committee allow the continued use of pesticides and chemicals during the storing and malting process so long as they comply with the Pesticides Precaution Scheme.

The Campaign for Real Ale (CAMRA)

CAMRA is a non-profit making consumer organization formed in 1971 to resist the threats to real ale. Its aims are to improve the drinking consumer's lot, both in the quality of what he drinks and where he chooses to drink it. It carries out one or two major campaigns a year. As traditionalists, CAMRA members are fighting for 'real' or cask conditioned ale, that is:

- Beer brewed from the natural ingredients of malted barley, water and hops;

- allowed to mature naturally in the cask in the pub cellar, and

- served in the traditional way, without the use of gas pressure.

CAMRA is run at a national level by an elected unpaid board of directors. It has over 150 branches in England, Wales and Scotland. It has a pub preservation group and a monopolies committee. The monopolies committee looks at all aspects of the structure and economics of the brewing industry and is especially concerned about local and national brewing monopolies and the way takeovers inevitably reduce consumer choice in beers. They also look at Government and EEC activities affecting the drinks sector.

CAMRA organizes a number of annual surveys. One of these charts the number of pubs 'lost' and 'gained' to real ale during the year. Around 50 per cent of pubs serve real ale compared with under 25 per cent when CAMRA was formed in 1971. The move back to cask-conditioned beer is gaining strength every year. Most of the country's major breweries now sell cask beer.

CAMRA Publications

- *The Good Beer Guide* (published annually).

- *CAMRA Dictionary of Beer.* Comprehensive guide to all British beer.

- *Whose Pint is it Anyway?* A call from the consumer for radical change in the brewing industry.

The above and a full list of publications are available from CAMRA head office.

CAMRA is probably one of the most successful consumer orientation pressure groups in the country, and its following increases yearly. Since 1971 the number of outlets for real ale has more than trebled. It shows what can be achieved when the consumer takes a positive and active interest in a subject. The same approach could work for the rest of the food we eat and drink. A 'purist' pressure group similar to CAMRA could monitor and survey the quality and production of food, to encourage the use of traditional methods and put an end to the use of unnecessary and harmful chemical aids and stimulants.

CAMRA Ltd, 34 Alma Road, St Albans, Herts AL1 3BW (Tel: St Albans 0727 67201).

Meat and the consumer

The number of consumers who prefer not to eat meat is growing steadily and among the meat-eating population many are not satisfied with the methods under which animals are reared. However, there are positive changes that could be implemented in the rearing of animals, such as a less intensive system of farming and the strict control of growth promoting agents. A new type of meat industry, one based on Soil Association Guidelines and Conservation Grade Standard, could possibly call itself the 'humanely produced meat industry'.

A hill farmer from West Yorkshire, who himself goes to great lengths to ensure that his family has meat free from as many chemicals as possible, changed from meat production to milk production some ten years ago. He is happy about his milk, but not entirely happy about the meat sold at present on the British market. When his own cows calve each year he keeps one or two calves as store cattle for his family. This is to ensure that he can feed them as he feels is right. No additives of any kind are used and only appropriate medication as directed by the vet. Mr Arkwright feels that the farming industry is ten years behind the health requirements of the consumer. He points out the anomaly that the Milk Marketing Board still continues to use high butter fat content of milk as a sign of quality. Until recently, he said, the Meat Federation also considered fat to be a sign of quality.

Arkwright, a pleasant man who goes about his work in a manner that agrees with his heart, believes many other farmers have great empathy with the land and their animals. Sadly there are others who see farming merely as a big business venture and use every cost-cutting technology on the market and every subsidy the EEC offers. They give farmers generally a bad name and the consumer feels little or no sympathy for genuine problems that the caring ones have to face.

Mr Arkwright believes that the food industry and meat production in particular is in for great changes over the next 10 to 15 years.

Meat does not carry a label listing ingredients. It is supposed to be just animal flesh, but as discussed in the section on hormones (see page 52) this is definitely not the case. The consumer is now actively seeking out meat that is drug- and additive-free. A number of butchers offer Soil Association and Conservation Grade meat. It is important to understand the difference between the two grades. Soil Association Grade meat is truly organic in that animals are fed and cared for using organic principles while Conservation Grade meat is produced using a non-chemical policy without drugs, and animals are kept in conditions conducive to their welfare.

Soil Association grade meat

At the moment truly organic meat is not available through any health food shop chain or supermarket. Safeways said that they were not ready to make a move on it until a consumer acceptable standard had been established. Soil Association grade meat principles are only beginning to be practised on farms. Small farms, smallholdings and farmers already producing organic vegetables, produce only limited amounts of SA grade meat, and supplies are therefore random and unreliable. It is time for meat farmers to introduce changes necessary to produce organic grade meat so that supermarkets can start offering this much desired choice to the consumer.

For details of individual farmers and small producers offering Soil Association grade meat write to the Soil Association, 86-88 Colston Street, Bristol BS1 5BB who will provide names and addresses. *The New Organic Food Guide* written by Alan Gear, executive director of the Henry Doubleday Research Association, also gives details of those offering SA grade meat and other organic, conservation and naturally grown produce in Britain and Ireland. It would be worthwhile collecting addresses of sources of organic meat and asking your local butcher to start stocking organic meat. It would then be up to you, the consumer, to continue to support him in providing the drug and additive free meat. When there is a demand a product will sell.

Conservation grade meat producers

These producers belong to the Guild of Conservation Food Production and have their own set of standards. For a full list of conservation grade farmers and outlets write to: Guild of Conservation Grade Meat Producers, Bedford Silo, Mile Road,

Bedford MK42 9TB (Tel: Bedford (0234) 327922). A number of companies offer Guild of Conservation Grade meat:

● **The Pure Meat Company** consists of a group of West Country farmers who belong to the Guild of Conservation Grade and advertise their meat as being without modern additives, chemicals and added growth hormones. They offer a range of beef, pork, poultry, bacon and ham using traditional methods of curing and smoking and a 19th century recipe for their sausages. Their prices compare very reasonably with regular butchers and they offer discounts on large orders. They assure quality and hygiene in their mail order system by using a vacuum packed process similar to the one used in transporting large pieces of meat to butchers. For further details of prices, etc., write to: The Pure Meat Company, 1 The Square, Moreton Hampstead, Devon (Tel: 0647 40321).

● **The Real Meat Company** is concerned about farm animal welfare, the irresponsible use of chemicals in animal rearing and the quality and purity of meat. The company aims to provide a link between discerning consumers and farmers prepared to rear their livestock according to the Real Meat Company's guidelines. It actively supports non-intensive farm systems and sponsors responsible, high welfare farming. The company was formed by two Wiltshire farmers, Gillian Metherell and Richard Guy, whose aim was to bring back a more traditional quality and taste to meat but also to protect the welfare of livestock. All livestock produced for the company are reared without the routine use of drugs. It sells a complete range of meats and meat products which interestingly changes with the seasons.

The range includes beef, poultry, pigs, lamb, bacon, ham, sausages, burgers, mince and sausages in natural skins. The company also provides a wide range of hand made cheeses, pies, a delicatessen selection and additive-free condiments. They offer a postal service using vacuum packs and a wide range of cuts at reasonable prices. The company sells to other butchers as well as running two shops of their own at Bath and Kingston upon Thames. For further details write to: The Real Meat Company Shop, 7 Hayes Place, Bear Flat, Bath, Avon (Tel: 0225 335139) *or* the Natural Foods Butchers Shop, 90 Elm Road, Kingston upon Thames, Surrey (Tel: 01-546 1556).

The following is a list of butchers and outlets which stock the company's products. Make sure that you request 'real meat' as they also sell meat whose history is unknown:

Gordon Bond, High Street, Lyndhurst, Hants	042128 2864
Artingstall, 32 High Street, Corsham, Nr Bath	0249 713253
D. & B. Jordan, 145 New Dover Road, Capel-Le-Ferne, Folkestone, Kent	0303 51119
Simon Harvell, The Butchers Shop, Iwerne Minster, Blandford, Dorset	0747 811229
Moore & Sons, 1275 High Road, Whetstone, London N20	01-445 2828
Thorogood, 113 Northfields Avenue, Ealing, London W13	01-567 0339
Strachen, 216 Sandycombe Road, Richmond, London	01-940 4697
J. Winslade, Kimber, 323 Horn Lane, Acton, London W3	01-992 1219
Highgate Butchers, 76 Highgate High Street, London N6	01-340 9817
Selfridges, Oxford Street, London W1	01-629 1234
Wrights, 10 Upper Green East, Mitcham, Surrey	01-648 3197
Brimarks, 90 Watling Street, Radlett, Herts	09276 6746
W. Buckingham, 63 Blythe Road, West Kensington, W.14	01-603 5170
Birdham Stores, Main Road, Birdham, Chichester	0243 512888
McElwee, 8 High Street, Arundel, W. Sussex	0903 882291
Grays, 2a St Martin Street, Wallingford, Oxon	0491 34158
Gibson & Coe, 49 George Street, Hove, Sussex	0273 731407
Brimarks, 241 East Barnet, London	01-449 5416
Caines, High Street, Cumnor, Oxford	0865 864366
Hearn & Son, 6 The Broadway, Chalfont St Peter, Bucks	0753 884883
Janes, 28 High Street, Sunninghill, Berks	0990 23534

Other contacts who can provide information about purchasing conservation grade meat and associated products:

Tolly Ltd,
4, Main Avenue,
Moor Park,
Northwood,
Middx

Grays Brothers,
2A St Martin's Street,
Wallingford,
Oxon

Organic Butchers,
217 Holloway Road,
London N7

Canvin International Ltd,
Meadow Lane,
Cardington,
Bedford
Beds
Tel: 02303 322

Messrs D. Holmes &
C. String,
Clint,
Harrogate,
Yorks

Byfords Butchers,
Leigh-on-Sea,
Essex

W.A. Lidgate Ltd,
110 Holland Park Avenue,
London W11

Woodlands Health Foods,
Woodlands West,

Harts Victoria Ltd,
39 Tashbrook Street,
London SW1

Gold Label Produce,
The Bowers,
Standon,
Staffs
Tel: (0782) 70435

F.A. & J. Jones & Son,
Red House Farm Butchers
Shop,
Spalford Lane,
North Scarle,
Lincoln LN6 9HB
Tel: 052277 224

Butchers Boy,
108 West Road,
Shoeburyness,
Essex

Marsh & Sons,
Redbourn,
Heath,
Herts

Dean Farm Shop,
Hemel Hempstead,
Herts

Hockeys Naturally,
Newtown Farm,

Frostenden,   South Gorley,
Wangford,   Fordingbridge,
Ipswich,   Hants SP6 2PW
Suffolk   Tel: 0425 52542
Tel: 050278 352

Although they have not yet started selling organic/conservation
grade meat Safeways may be worth writing to for an update on the
situation. Contact their head office at Safeway Food Stores Ltd,
Beddow Way, Aylesford, Maidstone, Kent ME20 7AT (Tel: 0622
72000).

Organic fruit and vegetables and the consumer

The days of the shrivelled organic vegetable are disappearing. With
marketing and distribution developing all the time there is a definite
improvement in quality. A full range of Organic Growers Association
packaging for bulk and retail sales has been developed for use by
members and their waving leaf symbol and 'Eat Organic' message
are familiar to the health food trade. With Organic Farm Foods (OFF)
organizing the wholesale distribution of supreme quality vegetables
enormous progress has been made. OFF now has depots in
Scotland, Lampeter in Wales as well as its office in Ipswich at Abacus
House, Station Yard, Needham Market, Ipswich (Tel: 0449 720838).
Availability will always remain seasonal, but imported goods from
reliable sources will fill the gap. Imports will come from such places
as Israel. During research for this book a tasting session of OFF
fruits and vegetables was organized and the general consensus was
that their taste and flavour was far superior to fruits and vegetables
grown using agro-chemical methods. The carrots and imported
grapes were considered to be of a quality not available in
supermarkets.

With reliable packaging techniques and efficient delivery services
we can expect to see an increase in fresh organic produce and its
regular availability in most health food shops, With clearer
guidelines and symbols becoming familiar to the general public,
supermarkets with an interest in healthier residue reduced foods

should also be routinely stocking fresh organic produce as Safeways do.

Organic cereals and the consumer

Cereals are one of the staple foods we rely upon for many of our basic nutrients. If we could guarantee that all our cereals were organically grown, it would make a major contribution to reducing the residue content of our diet. A number of growers/farmers produce cereals to Soil Association and Conservation grade and these are now becoming readily available in such supermarkets as Tesco's and Sainsbury's. The biggest breakthrough will be when the big national bakeries produce an organic loaf that is nationally available every day of the working week, that could be considered real progress.

The range of imported organic cereal products is also very good, but often available only in specialist shops. A number of organic gluten free products, such as millet flakes, maize flakes, rice flakes, buckwheat flour, couscous, and bulghur can be found for those on a special diet. Foodwatch is good for specialist cereals and has an ever-increasing range available through mail order or from its shop in Dorset (address at the back of the book).

Rice grown organically is becoming more readily available in health food shops but generally has not yet reached the supermarket shelves. The short grain Italian variety seems to be the one most frequently found. It provides an additional nutty taste and is excellent in risottos. Sadly, most brown rice on sale has been grown in an agro-chemical system and will contain more pesticide residues because the husk will have absorbed the pesticides. However, because of the obvious nutritional benefits of rice, particularly for diabetics, one should not give up eating it but actively seek and encourage the production of organically grown rice.

As breakfast cereals are generally produced from chemically treated basic ingredients, you would be advised to make your mueslis or granolas from trusted organic ingredients. A number of producers sell organic oats e.g., Moreflake, family millers since

1675 situated in Crewe, Cheshire CW2 6HP. Organic dried fruits and nuts are also available. Jordans, well known for cereals, offer a conservation grade special recipe muesli and are intending to increase their range. For details of their products write to: W. Jordans Cereals Ltd, Holme Mills, Biggleswade, Beds (Tel: 0767 318222).

Organically grown flour is by far the most readily available organic product on the market. Its versatility and relatively long shelf life make it a viable product to stock. If you are lucky, you may find several different brands, each offering a number of types of flour. Doves Farm provide an excellent range of organic flours including unbleached white, 100 per cent wholemeal strong for bread and a 100 per cent wholemeal fine milled which makes excellent pastries, and 100 per cent wholemeal fine milled self raising, which has transformed baking and creates feather-light sponges, small cakes and scones. Doves Farm also sell a range of cereals, but their most outstanding product is their digestive biscuits now being stocked by Sainsbury's and other shops at a reasonable price. For further details of their product range and stockists write to: Doves Farm Mill, Ham, Marlborough, Wiltshire.

The availability of organic wholemeal pasta is getting better all the time and pasta shapes are now appearing along with spaghetti, macaroni and lasagne. The Ugo and Waymill varieties are made in Britain, the Euvita and Lima ranges are imported. Organic buckwheat noodles are also widely available and are also suitable for those on a gluten free diet.

Legumes have yet to receive the organic treatment and so far there is no consistent source with a reputable producer's label. Foodwatch carries a range and your local health food shop may also be able to help.

The consumer wanting to know about the cost of conservation grade food will be satisfied to learn that generally speaking the prices compare with such stores as Marks & Spencer's, whose foodstuffs are not organic.

It is possible to join the Guild of Conservation Food Producers as a consumer member, whereupon you will be advised of product development and new information. Membership is £4 per annum. Write to: Guild of Conservation Food Producers, P.O. Box 157, Bedford MK42 9BY (Tel: Bedford (0234) 61626).

Growing your own

Once you have decided to enter the organic world you will find a wealth of information at your disposal and the pleasure of a whole new approach to cultivation.

Good, sound advice may be found at Ryton Gardens in Warwickshire, the national centre for organic gardening.

You will see vegetable cultivation, herb gardens, a bee garden, demonstrations of composting and natural pest control methods as well as unusual and endangered varieties of vegetables. For those who have not experienced organic food, a visit to the cafe serving organically grown food will provide the opportunity of savouring the difference in taste and texture. All sceptics in the food industry should visit Ryton Gardens. Afterwards, they might combine what they are practising with good sound ecological methods which a residue-conscious society will come to demand and expect.

One of Ryton's patrons is David Bellamy who endorses the view that: 'It is possible to produce and protect our crops and animals without risk to our own health and the destruction of wildlife. It is possible to maintain production of healthy food without the profligate use of oil-based fertilizers and the dangers inherent in the use of toxic chemicals.'

Ryton Gardens, Centre for Organic Gardening, Ryton-on-Dunsmore, Coventry CV8 3LG (Tel: 0203 303517).

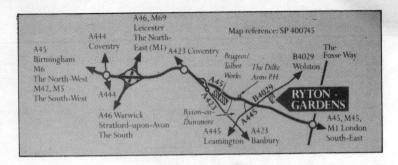

The Henry Doubleday Research Association

The Henry Doubleday Research Association (HDRA) is Britain's largest organic organization. It is a registered charity and was founded in 1958 by Lawrence D. Hills, who is now its president. The name is a tribute to Henry Doubleday, a 19th century Quaker inventor/smallholder who promoted the value of Russian comfrey as a fodder crop, plant fertilizer and medicinal compound. The Association still abides by his guidelines of 'searching for the truth that harms no man'. The HDRA has carried out some excellent projects. (Ryton Gardens is one of them.) The Association tries out new methods of safe pest control and encourages university students to carry out projects on their behalf. The findings are then passed on through their quarterly newsletter. If you wish to know more about HDRA you can contact them at the Ryton Gardens address.

Heritage Seeds

To grow modern F_1 hybrid seeds successfully it is necessary to use modern agro-chemicals. As we have already established, this method of agriculture leads to possible health risks. To reduce the risk to health we should not only buy organic foods but *grow* our own organic foods using varieties not dependent upon a barrage of agro-chemicals. Heritage Seeds seek to do this. Sadly legislation has seen over 1,000 varieties of vegetables fade away in the past six years.

Heritage Seeds have an interesting selection of seeds dating back to 1860. No seed treatment is applied and therefore growers are not exposed to possible contaminants. Their seed and complete organic gardening catalogue can be obtained from the address given for Ryton Gardens.

Organic Gardening Groups

Every gardener who realizes the dangers of modern chemicals will wish to keep them out of his own garden. Before modern chemicals were invented our fathers and grandfathers grew fruit and vegetables as good as any in our gardens today, using pest control methods which were safer for birds, bees and humans. Those who follow organic methods find that by building up a healthy, fertile soil and working with nature, plants develop a resistance to pests and disease. There is no need to use artificial fertilizers, pesticides and fungicides in the garden; many insects are repelled by the proximity of certain plants, and sprays can be made from others - especially some of the more aromatic herbs - and used as insect repellents. To learn more about these techniques you can join your local organic gardeners' group, name and address of which can be obtained from the Soil Association or the Henry Doubleday Research Association which also provides an organic gardeners' advice service.

The Centre for Alternative Technology

Another interesting place to visit, to investigate and absorb practical and sensible advice on organic growing methods. It is based at Machynlleth, Powys, in Wales.

Labels to look for

The Soil Association Ltd,
86 Colston Street,
Bristol
BS1 5BB

Soil Association Standard offers the consumer totally organic produce. This is the standard to which all others are compared. We have explained in detail on page 118 the Soil Association Standard. You will see this logo on paper bags, boxes and packaging.

Biodynamic Agricultural
Association,
Woodman Lane,
Clent,
Stourbridge,
West Midlands
DY9 9PX

The Demeter symbol used by members of the Biodynamic Agricultural Association stands for a system of agriculture which endeavours to achieve a dynamic balance between sound organic husbandry and planetary and lunar influences. It works upon the principle of the earth as a living organism in a living universe. This discipline was founded by Rudolf Steiner who in 1924 gave guidelines as to how these forces could be enhanced. The Association develops biodynamic preparations similar in formula to homoeopathic medicines. It operates a membership scheme and publishes a magazine along with conferences and workshops on biodynamic themes. The Demeter quality symbol is an internationally recognized symbol of organic quality.

The Farm Verified Organic
Information Centre,
86 Easton Street,
High Wycombe,
Bucks
HP11 1NB

(see page 124 for further details).
Products with this label are 100 per cent organic.

Organic Farmers and
Growers Ltd,
9 Station Approach,
Needham Market,
Ipswich,
Suffolk
IP6 8AT

OF & G Ltd distribute nationally to health food shops and large
supermarket chains. They have distribution centres in a variety of
areas including West Wales. They also stock a selection of foodstuffs
that are of intermediate grade i.e., not fully organic. If you would
like a more detailed explanation of this write to their address above.

Guild of Conservation Food
Producers,
P.O. Box 157,
Bedford
MK42 9BY

Tel: Bedford (0234) 61626

(see page 128 for details).

CHAPTER 6

Supermarkets

Most of the food we eat was bought at a supermarket. Bearing this in mind, the consumer needs to feel reassured that the food being sold there is of a high standard.

At one time in Britain we were only concerned with having enough food to eat. More recently doctors have told us to eat less fat, sugar, salt and additives and to eat more fibre. With these recommendations there has been a significant improvement in the overall health of some in the general population. Supermarkets have been instrumental in much of this change by increasing their ranges and availability of 'healthy' foods.

At one time the consumer could only buy wholemeal bread, legumes, vegetarian meals, brown rice etc., from a health food shop and would be considered cranky. Now that these foods are readily available and actively promoted by supermarkets using clear nutritional labelling, pricing them reasonably and providing recipe details, attitudes have changed. We hope to take healthy eating habits one stage further by encouraging the consumer to buy (or even grow for him or herself) organically grown produce.

The quality of the food you buy can in some cases be associated with your social class. Those who buy perfect and large items, are thought to be well off, whereas those who buy smaller, possibly blemished items are seen to be less well off. If we are to have foods without a residue content we must change our perception of quality. The consumer must learn to equate 'organic' with good quality. At present he or she may consider organic produce inferior because it is sometimes smaller and more irregular in shape and size than its non-organic counterpart; but it is a product that can be guaranteed residue free.

New varieties of seeds that grow well in soil rich in artificial fertilizer produce crops that take up a great deal of water. The result is watery, insipid produce lacking in flavour. Most of you have tasted home grown tomatoes. Mentally compare their flavour with commercially produced tomatoes available all year round! When produce is grown out of season it has to be 'forced' in some way. We are sacrificing real flavour for year-round availability.

There may be something to be said for returning to a seasonal way of life. The consumer has now become very blasé about the foods he buys and expects to be able to buy fresh strawberries in December. The reason why there are seasons has almost been forgotten – nature can only produce certain crops at certain times of the year when conditions are right. The consumer generally has lost the appreciation of the value of seasonal foods. Looking forward to spring after a long winter and a return to a more seasonal approach to foodstuffs would reduce boredom and increase appreciation. The consumer commands the buying power and he or she can exert a considerable influence over how our food is grown and manufactured.

Tesco

(Information provided direct from Tesco)

Every Tesco own label product is designed and produced to a Tesco specification which ensures safety, legality and product quality. Complex documentation details the methods of manufacture, quality control tests, and their frequency, microbiological standards and maximum limits for additives and contaminants. Additionally all products must, of course, conform to Government legislation and codes of practice.

In the course of a year Tesco laboratory analysts test over 22,000 products and carry out 168,000 analyses on these products. It also employs external laboratories to cover areas which it is not feasible to investigate in house, due to the cost of equipment. Its team of quality control technologists made over 6,000 visits to suppliers' premises in the course of a year, to ensure that specifications and codes of practice were being upheld. Here are quotes from Tesco's meat buying specification concerning contaminants.

'The use of illegal growth hormones, or indeed drugs prescribed by surgeons to treat animals where they are unaware that they are due for slaughter, is an area of great concern. Any evidence of livestock or carcasses having been adulterated by chemical contaminants is followed up to source and producers suspected of such practices are "blacklisted" as livestock suppliers for Tesco Stores Ltd. Where evidence is available of such practices it is offered to the relevant authorities and prosecution is encouraged.

'The use of antibiotics is still permitted but controlled here in Britain. We are aware of the concerns surrounding the potential development of antibiotic resistant bacteria such as salmonella. However, we can only insist on and monitor the adherence to the guidelines by ensuring that suppliers observe the minimum time between the last application and slaughter. In addition, we do as much laboratory testing as is practically possible, but we cannot sample every product, every day of every week. This policy applies to beef, pork and lamb.

'With regard to fish, and the rising levels of both sea and fresh water pollution we monitor periodically the levels of mercury, cadmium, lead and organochlorine residues.

'Hormones and other residues are concentrated in the organs of animals e.g., the liver, heart, and kidneys. This allows us to use the monitoring of offal products as sensitive indicators of any malpractice. Multi-residue analyses are complex, labour intensive and expensive, and we therefore use external expert laboratories to check the samples taken weekly from our produce range.

'Although there is no statutory definition in the UK of what constitutes an acceptable residue concentration, the maximum limits fixed by the EEC or recommended by the Codex Alimentarious Commission (CAC) of the UN Food and Agriculture Organization and World Health Organization are used as guidelines in this country.

' "Acceptable" residue levels have not yet been defined by regulations under the Food and Environment Protection Act (1985). Therefore at present the EEC, and CAC Maximum Residue Limits MRLs remain as guidelines only.

'The multi-residue analysis technique used has the ability to detect a possible 88 different pesticides. In particular we look for the following:

'Benomyl, Carbaryl, Dimethoate, Dithiocarbamates (Mancozeb, Thiram, Zineb), Iprodione, Metalaxyl, Permethrin, Quintozene, Tolclofos-methyl, Vinclozolin, Tecnazene, Carbendazim, Bromethane.

'We insist that suppliers use recommended levels as directed by MRLs and that the minimum time between the last application and harvest is strictly observed (14, 21 or 28 days).

'As regards packaging, all plastic films should conform to legislation and be approved for food use. We are aware of concern expressed in some quarters about the use of PVC film in contact with food but we have, as yet, no confirmation from MAFF of any grounds for this concern. We offer two types of film on sale to customers in our stores; PVC and polyethylene, and make specific reference on each pack to the fact they should not be allowed in contact with food during cooking.

'With reference to organically grown produce, we are trialling a range of organic vegetables at present (March 1987) in six stores. The products currently available are swede, onions, potatoes, green cabbage and leeks. We are hoping to introduce more lines to more stores if the trials prove successful. We have three suppliers in all who are approved by the Organic Farm Food Association and the Organic Soil Association. We make regular visits to these suppliers to take away samples which are then tested on our behalf by MAFF.

'In addition in 1986 we conducted an intensive survey on post harvested produce e.g., apples and from November 1986 we have been conducting a pesticide survey on imported citrus fruit in association with MAFF. Our data bank from research into residue analysis is, we believe, unique in the retail industry.'

Safeway

Details of Safeway's 'Organically grown' produce
provided direct from Safeway

'Organically grown' produce sold in Safeway is supplied only
by full symbol holders of the Soil Association in the UK, or
by growers outside the UK who conform to similar exacting
standards specified by the International Federation of Organic
Agriculture Movements (IFOAM) and carry brand names such
as Bio-top and Demeter.

'Organically grown' produce comes from land that has been
certified free from non-approved products for a minimum of
two years, and where a system of food husbandry is used
involving crop rotations and natural manures.

Safeway is offering the choice of 'Organically grown' produce
because it minimizes the risk of residues of modern pesticides,
particularly those that are known to persist in the soil. It meets
the needs of customers concerned about the excessive use
of crop treatments and abuse of the environment. Generally
'Organically grown' produce does not differ greatly in
appearance from conventionally grown crops. Apart from the
occasional visual blemish associated with growth in natural
conditions, one may also find evidence of pests which can
easily be washed off.

'Organic' producers often use old varieties of plants which
have the 'flavour of yesteryear'. Modern varieties too are
preferred in many taste panel trials if they have been
organically grown.

Because the crops are not being constantly sprayed with
modern pesticides, natural predators are allowed to thrive and
nature's balance keeps the pests in check. Some small number

of pests in the crop is inevitable but is treatable within organic guidelines.

All 'Organically grown' produce in Safeway carries a symbol to identify the product. Most of the produce is pre-packed to avoid mistaken identity. Any self selection produce is easily identified by small 'Organically grown' stickers on individual items.

Safeway makes regular checks on all growers using the 'Organically grown' label. All producers and importers must be members of the Soil Association which rigidly enforces the standards, and imported produce must conform to full IFOAM Regulations.

St Michael®

Marks and Spencer plc
(Information provided direct from Marks and Spencer)

Marks and Spencer policy is, and has always been, to develop and use whole, natural foods and ingredients, free wherever possible from additives.

All St Michael foods are produced to detailed specifications and manufacturing procedures which have been agreed between our suppliers and ourselves. Our relationship with our suppliers plays a key role in ensuring that, where pesticides and fertilizers are used they are handled professionally and that all guidelines and specifications are strictly adhered to. Additionally, we perform regular pesticide analyses on various products in the UK and abroad.

In rearing animals for St Michael foods, we demand high standards of husbandry and together with our suppliers, go to great lengths to avoid cruelty. We do not use hormones as growth promoters and antibiotics are only used to treat illness. In any case sufficient time is allowed for any chemicals to dissipate prior to slaughter.

As far as packaging is concerned, we are confident that none of the films we use are likely to be harmful to the health of our customers. In the case of high fat content foods e.g., cheese we use an alternative to stretch PVC with reduced additive migration.

In conclusion we employ a substantial team of food technologists who together with other members of our buying departments work closely with all our suppliers, government departments, and advisory bodies, to keep abreast of all the latest developments in food production, which will ensure the complete safety of food products we sell to our customers.

SAINSBURY'S

Sainsbury's

(Information provided direct from Sainsbury's)

Policy on Pesticides

The following points outline Sainsbury's position on the use of pesticides in the cultivation of fruits and vegetables.

Any consideration in relation to the use of pesticides in the cultivation of fruits and vegetables must be seen in conjunction with Sainsbury's marketing philosophy, which is to provide customers with the widest choice of the best quality products available at extremely competitive prices with overall concern for our customers' well-being.

Sainsbury's is in touch with interest groups and information services at all times to monitor issues that may affect products or services offered to customers.

At the current level of scientific knowledge it is not possible to produce fruit and vegetable crops of the quality and volume, at a price demanded by the customer without the use of a range of agricultural chemicals.

The great majority of our foodstuffs is bought under contract which enables Sainsbury's to set stringent detailed quality control specifications. In addition, our suppliers are required as a condition of supply to ensure that only pesticides covered by the Government approved chemical scheme are used and are applied at the times and rates prescribed. This is particularly important with regard to the safety period between pesticide application and the crop harvest which must be rigidly observed.

New legislation being introduced in the UK requires growers to maintain records of all pesticide applications, this is a requirement that for several years Sainsbury's has demanded of all suppliers.

On a day-to-day basis it is not possible for retailers such as ourselves to monitor continually potential chemical residues in fruits and vegetables, for example we have approximately 3,000 own-label food and drink lines alone from over 700 sources worldwide, in considerable tonnages.

However, our suppliers are visited on a regular basis by our technical staff to ensure the final product supplied is to the standard specified in every aspect. We also do not hesitate to arrange for any of our products to be examined either by ourselves or by reputable external laboratories if we consider there is a need.

Sainsbury's fully recognizes that it has a responsibility to ensure that any food we offer is not contaminated in any way that may affect our customers' health and well-being.

We are currently offering customers produce which has been 'organically' grown as a trial in 22 stores countrywide and will monitor the sales and interest in these products closely. It is worth noting that even with 'organically' grown produce, this does permit the use of certain naturally occurring chemicals.

Growth promoters
Any consideration of the use of growth promoters must be seen in conjunction with Sainsbury's marketing philosophy,

which is to provide customers with the widest choice of the best quality products available at extremely competitive prices with overall concern for our customers' well being.

At all times Sainsbury's is in touch with interest groups and information sources to monitor issues that may affect products or services offered to customers.

In the UK the use of growth promoters has become an integral part of cattle rearing and is of considerable financial benefit to British farmers, British consumers and the British economy.

The great majority of our foodstuffs is bought under contract which enables Sainsbury's to set detailed quality control specifications. In addition, there is a clear obligation on suppliers of meat to ensure that any growth promoters used are used only in strict accordance with Government requirements and EEC laws.

However, our suppliers are visited regularly by our technical staff to ensure the meat products are supplied to the standard specified. Also, we do not hesitate to arrange for our products to be examined either by ourselves or by reputable external laboratories if we consider there is a need.

Sainsbury's fully recognizes that is has a responsibility to ensure that any food we offer is not contaminated in any way that may affect our customers' health and well-being.

CHAPTER 7

Policies and politics

How the EEC affects the British consumer

● The EEC fixes the prices paid to the farmer for most food products and therefore affects prices in the shops.

● About two thirds of the EEC budget is spent subsidizing high farm prices and exports of EEC food surpluses which could otherwise benefit consumers.

● EEC laws such as the food labelling directive can help give more information to consumers about what they buy. But some laws favour producers at the expense of consumers e.g., producers do not have to disclose techniques used in growing and producing and can therefore use any means to produce an attractive product, the secrets of which are never revealed to the consumer.

The CECG (Consumers in the European Community Group)

This watchdog consumer group was set up in 1978 and is grant aided by the Department of Trade and Industry. It aims to represent and carry out research into EEC policies that affect UK consumers. Its member organizations include the Consumers Association, National Consumers Protection Council and Age Concern, England. Should you wish to make your views known about any aspects of the EEC write to the CECG at 24 Tufton Street, London SW1 3RB (Tel: 01-222 2662).

Until Britain has the equivalent of the USA's Environmental Protection Agency the majority of politicians are going to make decisions that are to their advantage and no one else's. What we need is an impartial third party to pave the way to a more balanced and rational future.

The Government and EEC policies

Policies need to change before health can improve. The Institute for European Environmental Policy at 3 Endsleigh Street, London WC1H 0DD (Tel: 01-388 2117) is an independent body set up for the analysis of environmental policies in Europe. It seeks to increase the awareness of the European dimension of environmental protection. From its beginnings in 1976 the Institute has seen its role as trying to help Parliaments and other policy making bodies to raise the quality of the European environmental debate and the implementation of environmental policy as an issue deserving top priority. A number of MEPs have taken up the issue of agriculture and the environment and are working towards a full Parliamentary resolution on the subject. At the time of going to press a report on the subject was being prepared by a Belgian Green MEP, Francois Roelants du Viver, examining the effects of modern agriculture on wildlife, landscape, soil and water and looking at the role of the Common Agriculture Policy (CAP).

In Britain the Government needs to recognize the importance of ecological and conservation matters and to start implementing workable policies. Our present Prime Minister as a chemist (and one of the team who developed a brand of soft, whipped ice-cream) is not psychologically in tune with ecological principles.

The Government has an employment problem which is apparently insoluble. Why not direct money and research away from military and defence to finding practical ways of cleaning up the environment? It could become a big growth industry!

The politics of food residues

Government policies have a tremendous influence on farming practices, which in turn affect our diet. The Health Education Authority now promotes lifestyles designed to reduce diet-related diseases. This interest in preventive medicine has taken many years to develop, but at last government money is becoming available for further research.

Unfortunately the same cannot be said to be true for research into the effects of chemical residues in food. This lack of interest was confirmed when we wrote to 20 MPs from all parties expressing our concern about chemical residues in food, and asking for their party's and their own personal view on this issue. We received replies from, among others, David Steel, Richard Livsey, Des Wilson and a letter on behalf of Edwina Currie and Norman Fowler, former Minister of Health and Social Services (and an acknowledgement slip from the Prime Minister).

The correspondence did not make us aware of any commitment on their part to solve the problem of chemical residues in food. Neither were we any clearer about their own or their party's policies on this issue. We did however receive a long letter from a civil servant at the DHSS on behalf of Edwina Currie and Norman Fowler. Below are extracts taken from the reply:

Turning to your general concern about the use of chemicals for pesticides this Government, like its predecessors, attaches great importance to safeguarding the health of humans and animals and protecting the environment by ensuring that pesticides can be used safely in this country. To this end the introduction of pesticides onto our market has been closely controlled for the past twenty-five years through the Pesticides Safety Precaution Scheme (PSPS). Under this the Government gives clearance for the marketing of a pesticide only if, after detailed scrutiny of the scientific data, it is satisfied that[1] provided the recommended precautions are followed, the product can be used without risk to humans. A company seeking clearance for any product is required to provide all the medical and scientific data needed for the purpose. This will include studies on the short and, where appropriate, long-term toxicity of the product, and on its cumulative effects, and on any delayed effects which might emerge after a latent period. The recommended precautions must appear on product labels. In granting or withholding clearance under the PSPS, Government is advised by the independent and expert Advisory Committee on Pesticides (ACP). This will include recommendations on the timing and rates of application to ensure that pesticide usage does not give rise to significant residues.[2] The PSPS includes provision for the use of any pesticides to be reviewed in the light of any new scientific evidence on risk, and over the years clearance for the marketing of various pesticides has been withdrawn as a result of such reviews.

In addition to the pre-marketing scrutiny of the Pesticides Safety Precaution Scheme, there are arrangements for monitoring pesticide residues in food.[3] Regular wide-ranging surveillance programmes are undertaken by acknowledged experts who form the Government's Steering Group on Food Surveillance's Working Party on Pesticide Residues (WPPR).[4] Such levels as are found in food in the UK are low, and for the basic commodities, generally well below the internationally accepted maximum residue limits. If you wish to know more about the results of its work you may want to read the Report is produced in 1986. The Report is available from your nearest HMSO and its reference is 'Report of the Working Party on Pesticide Residues (1982-1985). Food Surveillance Paper No.16'. MAFF. Cost = £5.00. Numerous studies undertaken for over twenty years have shown a steady decrease in the exposure of the UK population to those pesticides which give rise to residues in food and which might accumulate in the bodies of consumers.

As well as their concern with safety, it is the Government's declared intention to reduce pesticide usage to the minimum consistent with efficient food production.[5] The Food and Environment Protection Act, passed in 1985 now contains all the powers by Ministers to control the supply and use of pesticides. This is being used to strengthen and broaden current controls.

I understand that MAFF are giving much attention to studying the environmental impact of pesticides and the Agricultural Development and Advisory Service is engaged, with the co-operation of research institutes, in a great deal of research and development work on more efficient methods of crop protection and pesticide application. This includes studies on integrated pest management, the ecological effects of pesticides and the characteristics of spray-drift.

of pesticides and the characteristics of spray-drift. Biotechnology may also contribute to this area when further developments are effected in years to come.

It should be borne in mind, however, that every system of agriculture has disadvantages as well as advantages.[6] For isntance, organic farming is <u>less productive, more subject to crop failures due to pests</u>, at present requires the use of a certain amount of <u>man-made pesticides such as pyrethroids</u>, and if not done correctly <u>can be environmentally destructive</u>. Nitrates and phosphates for instance are essential for soil fertility and are obtained by planting and ploughing back legumes, or adding manure or using naturally produced nitrates and phosphates (e.g., bird droppings in Chile) or sewage sludge or slaughterhouse wastes.[7] There are <u>more offensive smells from treated fields creating a nuisance problem to nearby residents.</u>[8] Famines due to crop failures (e.g., potato famines) can arise when a <u>successful pest develops and spreads rapidly over large areas</u>. Husbandry is an important feature of organic farming and is another vulnerable link in the chain to successful production of crops.[9] <u>More research and development is needed if organic farming is to become more widely accepted</u>.

The toxicological testing and the various controls on the use of pesticides, hormones and antibiotics in meat production and on food additives are designed to ensure that food on sale is free from[10] <u>harmful levels of chemical substances. Labelling requirements have been introduced to ensure that purchasers can be aware of additives</u>, and a number of stores now market meat and other products which they guarantee to be free from additives, and vegetables which are organically grown. So, such products are available if not as widely as the generally accepted range of foods to those who wish to purchase them and are able to overlook the higher price and the authenticity of the product.

Finally, as far as diet is concerned ill health results from many factors, including poverty and unemployment and people everywhere can do a great deal to avoid ill health for themselves and their families by adopting a healthier lifestyle. The Government is in no doubt that the best way to prevent much of the ill health which afflicts this country is to ensure are mounting a number of new initiatives to inform the public about diet and health.

We have underlined and numbered a variety of quotes and statements from the letter. Here are our replies.

● **Quote: 'It is satisfied that provided the recommended precautions are followed, the product can be used without risk to humans'**
It should be firstly brought to the consumer's attention that the Government hardly ever makes it its business to check if users of pesticides are actually carrying out their recommended precautions. We have not come across any farmer or grower ever being prosecuted for malpractice, but because of the numerous incidents of inadvertent spraying of the general public we can assume that malpractices do exist. Those who use pesticides on farms and those in charge of pesticide application, often have little or no formal training. Due to lack of funds the inspectorate in charge of monitoring this area cannot perform a high level of service.

To say that poisons can be regularly applied to our food without risk, is both cavalier and incorrect. This type of statement remains unchallenged largely because nobody is adequately collecting the data and therefore no one as yet can act upon it. Let there be no disguising of the facts; there are no safe levels of pesticides nor any other toxic chemicals we find in use.

Dieldrin has been withdrawn as a result of these reviews – much too late in the day for many people who have specific illnesses as a direct result of dieldrin contamination.

● **Quote: 'Regular wide ranging surveillance programmes are undertaken by acknowledged experts who form the Government's Steering Group on Food Surveillance's Working Party on Pesticide Residues (WPPR).'**
This may be true but many of the people on these working parties work for those with vested interests, and so are unlikely to make unpopular decisions. Virtually no impartial work ever goes on in Britain.

● **Quote: 'Such levels as are found in food in the UK are low.'**
This is untrue. Friends of the Earth's report of 1984 on pesticides
and residues reveal that residues are significant and often above
the legal limits. In fact it could be said that there are no safe limits,
not even low ones.

From the investigations carried out in support of this report we
have no evidence to support this statement. We would even go as
far as to say that this statement is a 'red herring' and a falsehood.

● After receiving the letter from the DHSS we asked the hon.
general secretary of the Soil Association, Francis Blake, to comment.
Here is his reply:

Organic agriculture is a 'whole system' approach that
encompasses 'balance' and 'health' in all its principles. We
are what we eat, whether we are animal, vegetable or even
soil. In agriculture, this creates a direct link from soil through
plants, animals, humans, the environment in general and back
to the soil again. The health of one depends on the health
of each and on the balance throughout the whole. This is
recognized and embraced in organic systems, but is ignored
in conventional systems, with the consequences that we all
know.

The effects of organic agriculture therefore span at least three
government departments (MAFF, DoE and DHSS) and has
positive implications for all three. For MAFF, it could eradicate
the embarrassment and cost of CAP surpluses, and mend
the dreadful public image from which farming currently
suffers. It could enable farmers to produce food with a clear
conscience, using methods which are both sustainable and
safe. For the DoE, it could eradicate agricultural pollution of
the environment, whether from pesticides, nitrates, straw
burning or farm 'waste' (what a telling word that is), and resolve
the grievances of conservationists. For the DHSS, it could
dramatically improve the health of the nation, particularly
in the so called 'diseases of the 20th century'.

Unfortunately, government departments, by their very
nature, tend to exhibit extreme tunnel vision. It is often beyond
their capacity to appreciate or support something if its benefits
span more than one department. Organic agriculture is a

classic example. The one paragraph on organic farming in this DHSS letter could not have demonstrated their myopia, and in some instances their total ignorance, better.

● The lower productivity of organic methods is, in the current situation, a positive bonus.

● It is only government decree that has forced organic farmers to use man made pyrethroids – in sheep dips. They are not allowed in any other circumstances.

● '. . . if not done correctly can be environmentally destructive'. Conventional farming is far more environmentally destructive even when it *is* done correctly (e.g., nitrates in water supplies, pesticide poisoning, extinction of wildlife, etc.). When not, the consequences are even more terrible. There is no comparison.

● Chilean nitrate is not allowed in Soil Association Symbol production.

● Properly composted manures *do not smell*. It is usually the manures from conventional farms, which are not managed correctly, that smell offensively.

● The Irish potato famine would not have happened had proper rotations and other aspects of organic farming been employed. Monocropping, a common feature of conventional farms, was one prime cause. The balance inherent in organic systems is precisely the reason why pests and diseases are of minimal significance on organic farms.

● Husbandry is vital to all agriculture. Better applied to conventional farms, it would reduce considerably their dependence on chemical and poisonous inputs. Surely this should be a primary aim, not a feeble stumbling block?

● At last we have agreement. Organic farming desparately needs more research and development, for it currently enjoys neither support nor finance. Despite this, there are only minimal differences in yield. This fact alone suggests its tremendous potential, were it properly funded. The environmental and health benefits merely reinforce that potential.

It is ironic that the letter does not even mention the superiority of organic food in terms of nutritional status, lower chemical residues and general health-giving properties – the very areas in which the DHSS has responsibility. Small wonder perhaps, when it has only just discovered the link between diet and health. To make the connection between agriculture and food may be a bit too daring. Anyway, agriculture is out of its jurisdiction!

The DHSS would do well to get its facts right first, and then it might be in a better position to inform and to find solutions. The Soil Association is always ready to facilitate this process.

● **Quote: 'There are more offensive smells from treated fields creating a nuisance problem to nearby residents.'**
It is difficult to take this quote seriously. It is plainly obvious that the person making the comment has no knowledge of organic techniques, nor have they ever experienced the offensiveness of toxic fumes from crop spraying, or of other agro-chemical farming techniques.

See the reply from the Soil Association.

● **Quote: 'More research and development is needed if organic farming is to become more widely accepted.'**
Modest financial support for organic farms similar to that given to agro-chemically based farms, would enable them to offer the consumer a complete organic diet.

● **Quote: 'Free from harmful levels of chemical substances.'**
There are *no* harmless levels of chemical substances and the government is irresponsible in trying to suggest otherwise.

Watchdogs without teeth

Every local authority is legally obliged to have a public analyst. He or she is the first line of defence when it comes to protecting the consumer from contaminated food and drink. A public analyst has a degree in chemistry, is a member of the Royal Society of

Chemistry, and is completely familiar with all aspects of chemical analysis of food, drink and the environment.

Public analysts are not allowed to become involved directly or indirectly with any trade or business connected with the sale of drugs or food. Should a member of the general public wish to have a sample of food or drink analysed he or she will be charged a fee fixed by the local authority.

At their Annual Conference in 1987 the following lectures were an indication of the concern felt by public analysts about contamination of the environment:

● 'Aspects of local authority investigations into the safety and quality of the environment including air, water, land and radio-activity monitoring' by D.W. Lord, county analyst for Lancashire and Cumbria.

● 'Concern over the trace ingredients and contaminants appears to be growing. Is this justified and what controls are needed in the future?' R.S. Nicholson, regional chemist, Strathclyde.

● 'Is the level of control of food and consumer goods what the public expects?' D. Grose, Consumers Association.

Extracts taken from the Policy Statement 1985 prepared by The Association of Public Analysts states that:

'Recent experience has shown clearly that with the general cutback in local authority expenditure, all laboratories have found it increasingly difficult, and in many cases impossible, to meet the requirements which are fundamental to an effective service.'

It is alarming that public analysts are under such pressure that they feel unable to provide an adequate service to the consumer. They are the people who should and could highlight the risks to the general public – but due to lack of funds the necessary work by the public analyst will not be done. This report contends that the consumer is now having to take risks as a result of this situation.

Pesticides and the food gap

Farmers have always known that a percentage of their crops will be destroyed by pests. To be able to eat all year round the farmer needs to control the pests to provide himself with a comfortable surplus. Husbandry techniques were initially used: the manual removal of weeds, the growing of certain crops together (companion planting) e.g., growing pyrethrum marigolds next to tomatoes to keep aphids down. The use of insects as predators was encouraged e.g., ladybirds to control aphids.

The first recorded studies into the use of crop protection chemicals were in the mid 19th century. In the early 20th century several inorganic substances were developed and found to be effective against pests e.g., organomercury seed dressings were developed in Germany. Between the two World Wars, massive research generated a whole new chemical industry. The most significant find was the organo chlorine compound – dichlorodiphenyltrichloro-ethane (DDT) discovered in Switzerland, which was thought at that time to have great potential insecticidal properties. Work in Britain led to the development of 2,4,5-T (for further details see page 42).

The 1940s and 1950s were another period of development, with Europe and America leading the way. Many now familiar herbicides and insecticides were produced e.g., chlordane, malathion, carbamates (all insecticides) captan (fungicide) and finally paraquat (herbicide).

As an offshoot of the effort put into developing chemicals for pest control, scientists saw the potential of these new compounds as nerve gases. This led to continued research into nerve gases as potential pesticides.

These new chemical products, capable of controlling a wide variety of pests, were heralded as the answer to all the farmers' problems, helping to produce cheap food and ample supplies. They were used liberally over agricultural land throughout the western world in good faith. Farmers were totally unaware of the true implications of their actions.

It was only after the publication in 1963 of the book *The Silent Spring* by Rachel Carson that pesticides were seen in a completely different light. She was a biologist who simply documented her observations of the effects of pesticides on the American countryside. Although some factual errors were found in the book, the basic message that pesticides are potentially very dangerous and man uses them in the environment at his own risk is still true today. The book had a profound effect in the USA. It led to a ban on DDT and to a tightening up in the use of pesticides, and made the agro-chemical industry more responsible for its actions.

In the early 1970s population studies were showing an ever widening gap between population growth and food production. It was thought that by the year 2000 the earth's food crops would not be able to support the world's population. In response to this concern, research was channeled into developing new high yielding strains of basic crops that were disease resistant. This form of agriculture is very dependent upon large quantities of nitrogenous fertilizers being used, as well as the moderate use of pesticides. Farmers were very successful and yields were constantly improving, so much so that surpluses started appearing in the West. Grains were first to accumulate and require storing followed by milk, butter, cheese and beef mountains and most recently wine lakes. We have starvation in certain areas of the world but there still seems to be an inability on the part of the EEC to distribute food to those in need.

EEC Food Surpluses, February 1986

Skimmed milk powder	0.7 million tonnes
Butter	1.1 million tonnes
Cereals	15.3 million tonnes
Wine	3.5 billion litres
Storage costs	£360 million
Interest on storage costs	£470 million

A Statistical Guide To The UK Food System, The London Food Commission

Time to go less intensive

As a result of successive high production yields in farming, required cutbacks in milk and beef production has caused resentment and bafflement among farmers. There has been government pressure on farmers to continue with intensive farming methods, reduce supplies, sell off stock and redirect land use for forestry, leisure activities or housing. This attitude of actively encouraging an agro-chemically based farming system could result in even more pesticide residues in our food. We feel that we should be aiming for a continued reduction in the amount of agro-chemicals used in farming methods to the point where most of the food in Britain is residue free.

To achieve satisfactory levels of production without resorting to agro-chemicals we must ensure that as much of today's farm land remains in service as possible. Our hope is that any unused land should return to farm land. The techniques that would be environmentally acceptable would be a combination of good traditional husbandry management and responsible and minimal pesticide use.

A whole change in outlook is necessary to develop and maintain a satisfactory and safe farming system and this re-education should start in the agricultural colleges. The teaching of organic methods should become an integral part of the syllabus.

CHAPTER 8

The ecology lifestyle

Having an ecological lifestyle means realizing that we belong not only to a family and neighbourhood but also to a larger living world. How we go about our daily lives and interact with our environment has a bearing on the world as a whole. If we respect and aid nature, the natural world maintains its balance; conversely if we take out more than we put in and adopt short-sighted lifestyles, sooner or later the natural system will begin to disintegrate, since all our resources come from nature.

How you live your life will have a bearing on how your body interacts with the environment in which it finds itself. Sadly, those who are not in harmony are often those who suffer ill health, as happiness and a predisposition towards ill health are factors which may affect whether you develop for instance heart disease or cancer. For example, Personality A (defined as someone whose character tends towards aggression, obsession and competitiveness) may be the type of person already known to be more prone to coronary heart disease than Personality B (whose character is generally more relaxed and casual in its approach to life and its problems).

As research goes on finding links between personality type, environment and health and assessing their overall influences on us, we will know better how to change our lifestyles to reduce risk factors. This will take time as modern medicine does not readily consider environmental influences as possible factors in illness and is reluctant to pass on any known benefits to the general public until they have been categorically proven. For those of you who may wish to consider some ecologically based guidelines the following can easily be incorporated into busy lives.

● Detergents

The pollution caused by detergents was a problem largely of the early 1970s. Much was done to stop the foambergs in rivers and the consequent devastation of life in the water, but there are still problems. The phosphate content of washing-up liquids and washing powders can upset the delicate balance of nature by acting as a fertilizer, promoting growth particularly in the algae found in slow moving rivers, lakes and ponds. The algae overgrow, monopolizing most of the available space. This becomes a problem when the algae die and start to decompose. During this decomposition they de-oxygenate the water and the fish die along with other forms of oxygen-dependent water life. As re-establishing life in these dead waterways is always expensive and time-consuming the best way forward is to allow only biodegradable substances into the environment.

In Switzerland the use of phosphates is outlawed; in Britain the consumer can help by using biodegradable and phosphate-free cleaning agents that will not add to the problem. Ecover products are phosphate-free, biodegradable and environmentally safe. Products under the Ecover label – produced in Meerle, Belgium – are distributed in the UK by Full Moon Products, Charlton Court Farm, Steyning, Sussex. Their product range includes washing powder, wool wash liquid, washing-up liquid, cream cleanser, toilet cleaner, fabric conditioner, floor soap and a heavy duty hand cleanser for using after working on the car or in the garden. Two other companies offer ecologically based products. They are Faith Products, 52-56 Albion Road, Edinburgh, EH7 5QZ, and Caurnie, Canal Street, Kirkintilloch, Scotland (Tel: 041-776 1218). Faith Products are also found at 82 Great King's Street, Edinburgh, Scotland if you wish to find out more about their range of products.

The only drawback of these items is their cost. Although bearing in mind the fact that they are extremely concentrated products, they are still on the expensive side. What needs to happen is for a big company like Sainsbury's or Tesco's to market similar products, provide them with a suitable advertising image and subsequently bring the prices down by their usual methods of negotiating with a big company like Unilever to produce them on their behalf. We have already seen signs of forward thinking in Sainsbury's since they have started stocking System Q2 with the logo 'The science of safety'.

These products are non-toxic, non-caustic, non-abrasive, free from odour and colour additives and are environmentally safe. The brass cleaner we tried out in this range was excellent value and gave results we would have expected from any other metal polish. For further details of System Q2 write to Poly-Lina Ltd, Enfield, Middlesex, UK.

We are at present searching for an ecologically safe dishwasher powder/liquid. In our research we have come across a number of people suffering side effects from using the regular powders available.

- **Cosmetics**

This is an area where we could all make an ecologically sound contribution to the environment. Cosmetics are used for adornment and are non-essentials. The testing carried out for them is often performed on animals, although it is difficult to know which particular companies are the offenders. Some companies actively point out that their products are not tested on animals. The success of the Body Shop is an indication of how people feel about such issues. The company focuses heavily on the positive value of conservation, on minimal packaging, on animal welfare and on the use of natural oils, herbs and tinctures, at the same time providing excellent value for money.

- **Aerosols**

As concern increases over the effect of the propellants used in aerosols we can hopefully see a move away from the use of fluoro-hydrocarbons. They are used primarily because they do not react with anything 'chemically inert'. The USA have already banned them because consumers became concerned about the possible effect these hydrocarbons could be having on the ozone layer. It seems that by their use the delicate natural balance operating in the ozone layer can be altered or even broken down, thereby allowing more ultra violet rays through, excesses of which can lead to skin cancers, death of aquatic organisms and reduction in crop yields. As the USA have a policy of withdrawing any substance(s) known to be carcinogenic, they have stopped producing aerosols. However, as Britain never implemented the same discerning tactic we still have many products in aerosol form; even cream can be bought in an aerosol in a propellant of nitrous oxide (laughing gas).

● Waste

Waste and its disposal are also becoming a huge environmental problem. It is estimated that half the major cities in the USA will run out of their present tipping space in the 1990s. No one is prepared to make long-lasting unpopular decisions so we have a 'ticking over' situation at present.

Waste uses up energy in manufacturing processes and increases pollution. Almost half of all paper (42 per cent) used in the UK is devoted to packaging and eventually makes up one third of all household waste. The average Briton uses 105 bottles and jars each year but throws away 97 of them (or £350 million worth of materials in total!) Each year £4.5 million worth of scrap metal is buried and wasted.

Britain produces 43 million tonnes of rubbish every year. Each 2.5 tonnes of this waste could, if used, produce as much energy as one tonne of coal; yet we dump 90 per cent of our rubbish in holes in the ground. At today's coal prices the nation's rubbish is worth around £400 million and could keep 2.5 million families warm if it was burnt, but at present only six per cent is used as a source of energy. The Government admits that energy equivalent to 8.5 million tonnes of coal would be saved if Britain burnt its waste. However, only 10 energy recovery facilities have been built so far.

Several regional projects to produce energy from waste now operate. The Edmonton incinerator in North London burns 1,3000 tonnes of domestic and industrial waste each day. The heat produced is used to make electricity which is then sold to bring in £4.5 million. Newcastle and Sheffield City Councils are planning district-wide heating networks using refuse incinerators to generate heat.

The multinational 3M company has iniated over 50 clean-up projects in the company's UK operations and by eliminating wastes of all kinds has saved the company around £2.5 million. Globally, the policies adopted are estimated to have saved the company about £235 million.

Britain's recycling record is not good. Without too much effort, household output could be cut markedly. In 1986 only 28 per cent of aluminium was being recycled. Oxfam however has its own recycling centre, Wastesaver, which recycles clothing and aluminium. If only half the glass we used was recycled, 715,000 barrels of oil would be saved. The report of the National Council for Voluntary Organizations (NCVO), *Waste Recycling in the Community*, suggests that retailers, local and central government and industry should work together to develop a coherent national policy on recycling. Financial incentives should be given to local authorities to undertake recycling schemes; packaging companies should design products suitable for recycling; research into uses for reclaimed materials should be undertaken and supported, and markets created for recycled products.

You could introduce a compost heap in your garden, using it to put natural nutrients back into the ground as opposed to allowing organic waste to be burnt. There are numerous books available on how to begin a compost heap and introduce organic gardening methods.

As a consumer one can also refuse to buy products which are over-packaged, and complain to companies who indulge in extravagances of this kind. You can also make a point of supporting those companies who use materials which are biodegradable and who are receptive to ideas that the consumer knows to be environmentally safe.

Recycling would reduce the waste at our increasingly scarce landfill sites. It is up to you to support your community's anti-waste schemes or those of local voluntary organizations such as charity shops or Friends of the Earth. If you feel that your local authority should and could do more to encourage recycling write to your local councillors or local council encouraging them to set up anti-waste schemes such as bottle banks or monthly collections of paper, rags or sump oil for recycling or to use recycled paper for their stationery.

● **Fabrics**

The fabrics that we use today are becoming increasingly synthetic in origin. This is happening because of the need to keep costs down. Natural fabrics e.g., cotton, linen, silk and wool are more expensive to produce, and they are not without their risks. Cotton can, for example, have residues of pesticides left after spraying. Wool can have toxic residues left behind after the sheep have been dipped which can remain in the fibre. Those wearing garments with these remaining toxic residues could be absorbing poisonous chemicals through their skin. This is of particular importance with regard to baby clothes.

However, because there has not been any work carried out in this area and we consequently have no figures to go on this theory is, at present, purely speculative. For ecological reasons one could say that natural fibres should be more acceptable although one cannot be one hundred per cent sure that they are residue-free. Synthetic materials use a great deal of energy in their manufacture and may also cause pollution problems e.g., waste materials that are difficult to get rid of, fumes that are pumped out into the atmosphere.

● Energy conservation

It has become increasingly expensive to keep warm. Insulation is the way forward for the ecologically minded as it will soon be necessary to conserve fossil fuels. However, if you plan to insulate your home with cavity wall insulation be sure to investigate the materials that the installer uses. One of the possible materials is formaldehyde which should be avoided as there are possible health risks attached to exposure to formalin. Once the formaldehyde foam has been pumped into the wall cavity it sets quite firmly and is impossible to remove without knocking down the walls. Formaldehyde is a chemical that is used extensively and can be found in newsprint, plywood, plaster, tobacco, traffic fumes, setting lotion, cosmetics and contraceptives to name but a few. So if you react to your newspaper or become ill after having your hair done then you might be sensitive to formalin. For cavity wall insulation, go for more inert substances such as rock wall. For insulation generally, go for heavy curtains double glazing in non-plastic frames and a large dose of common sense.

David Stephens a consultant in the building sciences, has developed several new approaches to saving energy in houses by looking critically at the physics of buildings and human needs. The techniques he has developed can be used in any house but are especially valuable in old solid walled houses which are often damp.

Mr Stephens recently acquired a site at Rhayader in Mid-Wales on which to build a solar village of about 90 houses as a private enterprise development. Several different types of low energy houses are proposed but predominant would be passive solar heated houses with a greenhouse roof. Mr Stephens can be contacted at Practical Alternatives, Victoria House, Bridge Street, Rhayader, Powys LD6 5AG (Tel: 0597 810929).

• Lead

The campaign to remove lead from petrol has been with us for a number of years. Dr Derek Bryce-Smith, an ardent campaigner for the removal of lead in petrol, carried out many studies in this area. In 1987 television adverts with the vivacious Anneka Rice proved that ecologically sound products can take off when they are brought to the public's attention by a well-known personality.

Lead pollution is not entirely attributable to emissions from exhausts, however. It is likely that smokers accumulate more lead, along with cadmium, faster in their bodies than other people because cigarettes are heavily laden with these and other toxic heavy metals. This makes smokers more liable to develop lung cancer, heart disease, emphysema and stomach cancer. Thankfully the smoking of cigarettes is on the decline and smokers are now being asked to practise their habit in places away from everyone else. Those most vulnerable to the effects of passive smoking are babies and young children because they have no control over their surroundings. They should expect priority attention from those who care for them.

If you live in an area where the houses were built before World War II or live on the fringe of an old established area your water probably passes through lead pipes to get to your home. During the night the water will remain stagnant and therefore some of the lead from the piping will dissolve in it. This will then be drawn off in your home and you could be unknowingly making your early morning cuppa from water rich in lead. If you were brought up in times when lead was the only piping material you would have been told to run the taps for at least five minutes first thing every morning. This habit has largely disappeared. Although not very good in the conservation of water it is a sound preventive measure if you still have lead pipes, because with our 'improved' sanitation system many do not believe that water contains anything remotely dangerous. Sadly this is far from the truth.

Those most at risk are babies and young children, the chronically sick, the elderly and those who are sensitive to the heavy metals that they may have absorbed. So long as no one actually is seen to die from polluted or contaminated water no one is going to do anything – so it's up to you.

What can you do? Turn to the section on nitrates, page 72 for details of water filtration systems. Most offer a reasonable level of protection from lead. You should also make your views known to your local MP and water authority. Safe water is a basic right and necessity.

● Food

If you would like to be able to buy food produced along ecologically sound principles then you must be prepared to support companies who provide it, and keep asking others to provide it too. You may also feel inclined to withdraw your buying power from shops, supermarkets and companies that in your opinion do not uphold ecological principles. You may want to write to those you do patronize to find out their policies and views. We have asked some of the leading manufacturers for their practices and policies on a variety of ecological matters and after reading their replies you may or may not feel satisfied with their attitudes and outlook. You as the consumer could encourage (or pressurize) them to take a fresh look at this area. Without you they will fail to survive.

To become more discerning consumers, we need to learn to read between the lines. It is rather an uncomfortable feeling to know that you have been taken for a ride. To judge a product critically when rushing is difficult but not impossible. A number of well written, balanced books can help to sharpen judgement: *The Living Soil* by Lady Eve Balfour, Faber, 1943; *A Month-by-Month Guide to Organic Gardening* by Lawrence D. Hills, Thorsons, 1983; *A New Look at Life on Earth* by J. Lovelock, Oxford University Press, 1979; *Friends of the Earth Handbook*, Macdonald, 1987 and *Blueprint for a Green Planet* by John Seymour and Herbert Giradet, Dorling Kindersley, 1987. The London Ecology Centre, 45 Shelton Street, Covent Garden, London WC2H 9HJ is also worth a visit.

A residue-reduced lifestyle

By gaining a full profile of your own health and the health of other individuals in your family you can arrange a lifestyle to suit your own personal needs. The book *Detox* by Phyllis Saifa and Merla

Zellerbach, ISBN No: 87477-332-6 tells you how to clear out toxic material from the body. A visit to Doctor Jean Monro's hospitals for environmental medicine would also be of value. Once you have established a balance within your own system, then eating organic foods on a rotational system and using filtered or bottled water should provide some measure of protection against the adverse effects of toxic residues.

Living residue-reduced is difficult because of the pollution we experience in our cities and countryside. We have to be particular about where we live and what chemicals we introduce into our homes. When you need to maintain or redecorate your home, choose more carefully and consider the chemical components of materials used.

You will not feel instantly better from all of these changes, but over a period of time your body will stop reacting allergically to many everyday chemicals and foods, your general health will improve and you will develop a resistance to illness in general. Any symptoms you endure as a result of any allergic reaction will subside into the bargain and you will be able to look forward to a better quality of life and possibly a longer one.

The way forward

No matter what you are told, there are no safe levels of residues. Everyone reacts differently to new and foreign bodies in their system and therefore with each person you are dealing with an unknown situation. This is completely and utterly unacceptable. Those most at risk in the healthy population are babies, particularly premature babies and young children. Much of the illness we now see is caused by environmental factors, a new and difficult concept to come to terms with. You the consumer, will be the one to become ill. Therefore it is important to tell food suppliers, decision takers and policy makers in this country to get their houses in order. We want to exercise our right to choose, to enjoy better health, and we demand that those in charge provide us with the necessary means and ways.

When the change comes – as it will because we will *not* be ignored – a healthier, happier, more prosperous generation will arrive and we will look back on the past 50 years as a time of misguided, floundering despondency. We must free our trapped selves from within the residue reservoirs of ill health. Once freed, cleansed and detoxified we can start to rebuild the world. We will have learned never to misuse it again as it was in the mid 20th century.

Useful addresses

Foresight (The Association for the Promotion of Preconceptual Care), The Old Vicarage, Church Lane, Witley, Surrey GU8 5PN (Tel: Wormley (042879) 4506 between 9.30 a.m. and 7.30 p.m.).

London Food Commission, 88 Old Street, London EC1V 9AR (Tel: 01-253 9513).

Dr John Mansfield, The Burghwood Clinic, 34 Brighton Road, Banstead, Surrey SM7 1BS (Tel: Burgh Heath (07373) 61177).

Dr Jean Monro, Sunbury Hill Clinic, Allergy and Environmental Medicine Hospital, Breakspear, High Street, Abbots Langley, Hertfordshire WD4 9HT (Tel: 09277 61333).
and: The Lister Hospital, Chelsea Bridge Road, London SW1W 8RH (Tel: 01-730 3417).

Henry Doubleday Research Association (HDRA), National Centre for Organic Gardening, Ryton on Dunsmore, Coventry CV8 3LG (Tel: Coventry (0203) 303517).

Soil Association, 86/88 Colston Street, Bristol BS1 5BB (Tel: Bristol (0272) 290661).

Friends of the Earth, 26/28 Underwood Street, London N1 7JQ (Tel: 01-490 1555).

Action Against Allergy, 43 The Downs, Wimbledon, London SW20 (Tel: 01-947 5082).

National Anti-Fluoridation Campaign, 36 Station Road, Thames Ditton, Surrey KT7 0NS (Tel: 01-398 2117).

National Childbirth Trust, 9 Queensborough Terrace, London W2 (Tel: 01-221 3833).

Environmental Medicine Foundation, Registered Charity. Researches into illnesses caused by environmental problems, Hon. Secretary Mrs J. Collett, Furnival House, 14-18 High Holborn, London WC1V 6BX.

'Foodwatch', Butts Pond Industrial Estate, Sturminster Newton, Dorset DT10 1AZ.

Commonwealth Institute of Biological Control, 56 Queen's Gate, London SW7 5JR (Tel: 01-584 0067).

Herb Society, 77 Great Peter Street, London SW1P 2EZ (Tel: 01-222 3634).

McCarrison Society for Nutrition in Health, 36 Bowness Avenue, Headington, Oxford OX3 0AL (Tel: Oxford (0865) 61272).

National Pure Water Association, Bank Farm, Aston Pigott, Westbury, Shrewsbury SY5 9HH (Tel: Worthen (074-383) 445).

Templegarth Trust, 82 Tinkle Street, Grimoldby, Louth, Lincs LN11 8TF (Tel: South Cockerington (0507-82) 655).

International Institute of Biological Husbandry (IIBH), Abacus House, Station Approach, Needham Market, Ipswich, Suffolk (Tel: Needham Market (0449) 720838).

The Conservation Society, 12a Guildford Street, Chertsey, Kent KT16 9BQ.

Organic food: where to find it

Organically grown vegetables are widely available, but organic meat, cow's milk, poultry, eggs and wine are a little more difficult to obtain. Here are some outlets which may also be useful if you have a business and would like to stock organic foods.

Area	Address	Tel. No.	Foods/Facts available
Avon	John and Janet Arnold Hollycroft, Winscomb Hill, BS25	093-484-2578	Vegetables, soft fruit, apples, eggs, meat, salad crops, honey, most P.Y.O.

Area	Address	Tel. No.	Foods/Facts available
Avon	Radford Mill Farm, Tinsbury, Nr Bath		Vegetables, dairy produce, eggs, meat, fish
Avon	Shop in Bristol — 41 Picton Street, Montpelier, Bristol 6		
Avon	Real Meat Company's Shop, 7 Hayes Place, Bath		Meat and meat products
Bedford	Guild of Conservation Grade Producers, Bedford Silo, Mile Road, Bedford MK42 9TB	0234 327922	Meat, poultry, game, list of suppliers
Berkshire	Vintage Roots, 88 Redstock Road, Reading, Berks RG1 3PR (postal service)	0734 662569	Organic and vegetarian wine suppliers
Berkshire	Dr Peggy Ellis, Little Bottom Farm, c/o 64 Blenham Road, Caversham, Berks RG4 7RS	0734 47157 Evenings only	Eggs, hens, honey, herbs, meat, soft fruit, grown to order and P.Y.O. by arrangement
Buckinghamshire	The Organic Wine Company Ltd, P.O. Box 81, High Wycombe, Bucks HP11 1LJ (postal service)		Organic and vegetarian wine suppliers
Channel Isles Guernsey	Lt. Col. P. A. Wooton, Le Rouvets Tropical Gardens, Perelle, St Saricans, Guernsey, C.I.	0481 63566/ 64345	Vegetables, salad crops, seville oranges, limes, grapefruit, lemons, pineapples, bananas, cherries, papayas and other tropical fruits
Cumbria	N. and A. Jones, The Watermill, Little Salkeld, Penrith, Cumbria CA10 1NN	076 881 523	Goat's and cow's milk, honey, vegetables, flour and cereals. Open Easter — September Weds, Thurs, Sun. 2.30-5.30 phone if not sure
Derbyshire	Mrs A. Hughes, The Priory, Woodeaves, Fenny Bently, Nr Ashbourne, Derby	033 529 238	Pork, lamb, mutton, poultry, honey, eggs, hens and ducks
Devon	I. J. G. McGregor, Lower Longcombe Farm, Totnes	Totnes 863259	Watercress and leeks

Area	Address	Tel. No.	Foods/Facts available
Devon	Morrish, East Ackland Farm, Landkey, Barnstable, EX32 0LD	Swimbridge 216	Beef, lamb to order, swedes and Bramleys
Devon	Ian Neilson, Wooladon Farm, Lifton, Devon	056 684 271	Lamb, beef, for the freezer. Wholewheat and barley 50 lb bags
Devon	The Pure Meat Company, 1 The Square, Moreton Hampstead, Devon	0647 40321	Mail order. Meat, game, poultry
Devon	Mr and Mrs Willcocks, Higher Birch, Bone Alston, Yelverton PL20 7BY	0822 840257 after 5 p.m.	Beef quarters, whole lambs for the freezer
Dorset	Foodwatch, Butts Pond Industrial Estate, Sturminster Newton, Dorset DT10 1AZ	0258 73356	Wide variety of specialized foods
Essex	R. Smith, Newhouse Farm, Rodwinter, Saffron Walden, Essex		Potatoes, lamb, beef produce to order
Gloucestershire	Mr and Mrs D. J. Beer, 'Gilberts', Brookthorpe, Nr Gloucester GL3 0UM	0452 812364	Honey, eggs, veal, lamb, Christmas cocks, hard/soft cheese, fruit and vegetables
Gloucestershire	A. Rennie, Cotswold Mushrooms, Garricks, Andoversford, Glos.	024 282 764	Mushrooms
Hants	Mrs C. Ashby, Coronation Cottage, Main Road, East Boldre, Brockenhurst, Hants	059 065 336 after 6 p.m.	Pork, eggs, cream, honey
Hampshire	P. and C. Hockey, Newtown Farm, South Gorley, Fordingbridge, Hants SP6 2PT	0425 52542	Beef, chickens, eggs, lamb, meat products, trout Tues-Sat 9a.m.-6p.m. Fri 9a.m.-7p.m.
Hampshire	B. and P. Hooker, Southview Farm, Duckpond Lane, Blendworth, Portsmouth, Hants PO8 0AP	0705 595805	Free range pigs to order, rabbits, chickens, dairy produce, goat's produce, eggs (duck and hens), vegetables, soft fruit
Kent	M. G. D. Smith-Cowfer, Westwood Farm, Kingston, Nr Canterbury, Kent CT4 6JN	0227 830811	Beef, pork, organic cream, cottage cheese, eggs, fruit, vegetables, honey

Area	Address	Tel. No.	Foods/Facts available
Kent	Safeway Food Stores Ltd, Beddow Way, Aylesford, Kent (write to this address for your nearest Safeway supermarket)	0622 72480	Sell a wide range of organic foods
Lincolnshire	F. A. Jones and Son, Road House Farm, Spalford Lane, North Scarfle, Lincoln LN6 9HB	052 277 224	Additive-free pork, beef, chickens, eggs, meat products. Open Wed-Sat 9a.m.-12.30p.m. and 1.30p.m.-5p.m., Fri until 7p.m. Sun 10.30a.m.-4p.m.
Lincolnshire	Lincolnshire Wine Company, Chapel Lane, Ludborough, Grimsby DN36 5SJ (postal service)	0472 840858	Organic wine suppliers
London	Wholefoods of Baker Street, 31 Paddington St, London W1 *and* 24 Paddington Street, London W1	01-486 1390	Meat, poultry, meat products, general wholefoods. Closed Mondays
London	Tasty Bits, 31 Barrington Road, London N8 8QT	01-340 2413	Meat and other additive-free foods
London	J. Sainsbury plc, Stamford House, Stamford Street, London SE1 (write to Liz Young at above address for details of current list of organic products)	01-921 6000	Organic vegetables in some stores (22 nationwide). Dove Farm household products which are organic are also appearing
East and West Midlands	D. S. Clement and Sons, Broome Farm, Broome, Stourbridge, W. Midlands	0562 700274	Potatoes
Somerset	R. Colling, Little Burcott Farm, Burcott, Nr Wells, Somerset BA5 1NG	0749 72091	Beef, lamb, pork, cider, guernsey milk and cream
Suffolk	Organic Farmers and Growers Ltd, Abacus House, Station Approach, Needham Market, Ipswich, Suffolk IP6 8AT		Details of growers
Suffolk	Sykes & Popham, Church Farm House, Hawstead, Bury St Edmunds, Suffolk IP29 5NT	028 486 596	Untreated Cox's apples, milk, cream, skimmed milk, eggs, vegetables, meat produced to order
Surrey	C. Gilliam, Birketts Farm, Tanhurst Lane, Holmbury St Mary, Dorking, Surrey	030 570 348	Beef, lamb, pork, eggs

Area	Address	Tel. No.	Foods/Facts available
East Sussex	Mrs J. F. Flintan, Flintan Farm Enterprises Ltd, Shepherd's Hill, Buxted, E. Sussex TN22 4PX	Framfield 340	Meat, veal, bacon, goat's milk, untreated Jersey milk, poultry for allergy sufferers
East Sussex	D. and H. Kiley-Worthington, Milton Court Ecological Farm and Stud, Polegate, E. Sussex	0323 870890	Beef, lamb, pork, poultry, milk, cream, dairy produce
West Sussex	Springhill Farm Foods Ltd, House Lane, Steyning, W. Sussex BN4 3DF		Cereals, beans, peas, lentils, dried goods
West Sussex	The Organic Food Company Ltd, Steyning, West Susex		Organic coffee 'Cafe Organico' from a Dutch company — Simon Levelt
West Sussex	Living Foods, P.O. Box 66, Chichester, W. Sussex PO18 9HH	070 131 226	Organic soya milk and rice cakes and other wholefoods
Tyne and Wear	Redesdale Sheep Dairy, Soppitt Farm, Otterburn, Northumberland	0830 20276	Sheep dairy
Wales	Mr W. Orchard, Poultry Farm, Penyrheol, Caerphilly	Caerphilly 882183	Antibiotic and hormone-free eggs. (Trade name: Mr Welshegg)

References

This section contains references, quotes, extracts and references to television programmes and suggested further reading. Each chapter has been dealt with separately. Details of sources and supporting scientific material have been given as documentation of all work put forward. Also included are issues that need more investigation without the restrictions of the Official Secrets Act or commercial constraints.

Introduction

Further reading:

C. Walker and G. Cannon: *The Food Scandal* (Century, 1985).

David Bull: *A Growing Problem. Pesticides and the third world poor* (1982).

Europe's Mountain of Injustice: *The Western Mail*, Wales (April 8, 1987).

Abstract: While another 15 million people will die of starvation this coming year, staggering quantities of stored food are rotting and being destroyed. Llewellyn Smith MEP for South East Wales, highlights what he calls 'the obscenities of the EEC food mountains'.

Policies and politics

Geoffrey Cannon: *The Politics of Food* (Century, 1987).

S. Epstein: *The Politics of Cancer* (Anchor Books, New York, 1979).

L. Doyal, K. Green, A. Irwin, D. Russell, F. Steward, R. Williams, D. Gee and S. Epstein: *Cancer in Britain – the politics of prevention* (Pluto Press, 1983).

Pesticides

R. Carson: *Silent Spring* (Hamish Hamilton, 1963).

Pesticides. Reference book 500 – MAFF Health and Safety Executive, 1986. ISBN 0 11 242782 0.

Lists pesticides approved under the control of pesticide regulations 1986. Contents include: *Herbicides* including growth regulators, defoliants, rooting agents and desiccators; *Fungicides* including bactericides; *Insecticides* including acaricides and nematicides; *Vertebrate control products* includes rodenticides, mole killers and bird repellents; *Biological Agents*; *Miscellaneous* includes synergists, molluscides, lumbricides, soil sterilants and fumigants; *Parallel imports*; *Substances sold for pesticidal and non-pesticidal uses*; *Active ingredients index*; *Product trade name index*; *HSE Approved list*; *Wood preservatives* and *Masonry biocides*.

Pesticide poisoning. Department of Health and Social Security. ISBN: 0 11 320830 8 (Re-printed annually).

Page 38: Organochlorine Compounds; uses; routes of absorption; pharmacology and toxic effects; management and treatment.

Page 39: Organophosphorus compounds; uses; routes of absorption; pharmacology; toxic effects; management and treatment.

A booklet set for Medical Practitioners on symptoms, diagnosis and treatment of *acute only* poisoning – gives trade names, active ingredients and pesticide class.

Further reading:

Richard Mackarness: *Chemical Victims* (Pan, 1980).

R. Van Den Bosch: *The Pesticide Conspiracy* (Prism, 1980).

C.G. Wright and R.B. Leidy: 'Insecticide Residues in the Air of Buildings and Pest Control Vehicles', *Bulletin of Environmental Contamination and Toxicology* (Vol. 24, pp. 582-589, 1980).

Merrill D. Jackson and Robert G. Lewis, 'Insecticide Concentration in Air after Application of Pest Control Strips', *Bulletin of Environmental Contamination and Toxicology*, Vol. 27, pp. 122-125 (1981).

C.G. Wright, R.B. Leidy and H.E. Dupree Jr, 'Insecticides in the Ambient Air of Rooms Following their Application for Control of Pests', *Bulletin of Environmental Contamination and Toxicology*, Vol. 26, pp. 548-553 (1981).

E.O. Dillingham and J. Autain, 'Teratogenicity, mutagenicity and cellular toxicity of phthalate esters'. *Environment Health Perspect*, 3:81 (1973).

IARC Report: *On Evaluation of Carcinogenic Risk of Chemicals to Man* (United Nations World Health Organization, Leone, France, 1972). International Agency for Research on Cancer Monograph, available from the American Public Health Association, Inc, Washington, D.C.

C.D. Klaassen and G.L. Plaa: 'Relative effects of various chlorinated hydrocarbons on liver and kidney function in dogs'. *J. Appl. Pharmacol.*, 10:119 (1967).

I.R. Politzer, S. Githens, B.J. Dowty and J.I. Laseter: 'Gas chromatographic evaluation of the volatile constituents of lung, brain and liver tissues', *J. Chromatogr. Sci.*, 13:378 (1975).

A.B. Robinson, D. Partridge, M. Turner, R. Teranishi and L. Pauline: 'An apparatus for the quantitative analysis of volatile compounds in urine'. *J. Chromatogr.*, 85:19 (1973).

J. Vessman and G. Rietz: 'Determination of di(ethylhexyl) phthalate in human plasma and plasma proteins by electron capture gas chromatography'. *J. Chromatogr.*, 100:154 (1974).

Committee on Toxicology National Research Council in assessment of the health risks of seven pesticides used for termite control – National Academy Press, Washington D.C., page 6 (1982).

P. Snell and K. Nicol: *Pesticide Residues and Food – The case for real control* (London Food Commission, 1986).

Television programme, December 1987 on HTV Wales, Culverhouse Cross, Cardiff. Producer Chris Seager examined the links between

Lindane sprayed by Rentokil in the home of a young boy who developed aplastic anaemia (Further reading – 'Aplastic anaemia following exposure to benzene hexachloride' (Lindane) – J. Phillip Loge MD *JAMA*. July 12th 1965, Vol. 193 No. 2. From the University of California Centre for Health: Reprints from: 575 West Fifth Street, San Bernardino, California, USA.

J. Erlichman: *Gluttons for Punishment* (Penguin, 1986).

Analysis of Herbicides – Determination of herbicide residues in agricultural crops – food – soil – water by chromometric method, Research Inst. ChemTee Bratislaca, Czechoslovakia, Nutrition Abstracts and Reviews, Series A. Human and Experimental, Vol. 57, No. 10 (October 1987).

J. Crocker et al: *The Lancet*, ii 22 (1974).

de Vlieger et al: *Archives of Environmental Health*, 17-759 (1968).

F. Duffy et al: *Toxicology and Applied Pharmacology*, 47-161 (1979).

M. Fielding and H. James. In *Food and Environmental Factors in Human Disease* (1984). British Society for Clinical Ecology, p. 102.

R. Finn: *Clinical Nephrology*, 14-173 (1980).

Pesticides – The First Incidents Report, Friends of the Earth (1985).

L. Greene et al: In *Food and Environmental Factors in Human Disease*, British Society for Clinical Ecology, p. 111 (1984).

W. Hallenbeck, et al: In *Pesticides and Human Health* (Springer, 1985).

M. Johnson: *Critical Reviews in Toxicology*, June Ed. 289 (1975).

R. Nicolson: *Journal Association Public Analysts* (1984), 22-5157 (1987).

D. Wilkin and Fishwick – Proceedings of British Crop Protection Conference, 183 (1981).

J.B. Cavanagh: *Peripheral neuropathy caused by toxic agents*, CRC – *Critical Reviews in Toxicology*, 2-365 (1973).

Arthur J. Riopelle and David G. Hubbard: *Pesticides cause lack of manganese. Prenatal manganese deprivation and early behaviour of primates.*

A.M. Andrew: 'Abnormal reactions and their frequency in cattle following the use of OP warble fly dressing', Veterinary Department, Meat and Livestock Commission, P.O. Box 44, Queensway House, Bletchley, Milton Keynes. *Veterinary record*, pp. 109, 171, 175 (1981). (*Conclusion:* The following was recorded as observations in the same group – increased salivation, general unease, muscle twitching, head swinging from side to side.)

D.V. Roberts: *Pharmacology and toxicology of OP pesticides.*

F.H. Duffy, J.L. Burchfiel: *Long term effects of the OP's Sarin on EEG's in monkeys and humans*, Children's Hospital, Harvard Medical School, 300 Long Wood Avenue, Boston, Massachusetts 02115.

Duffy, Burchfiel, Bartels, Gaon, Sim et al: *Long-term effects of an OP upon human EEG*, Seizure Unit, Neurophysiology Lab., Children's Hospital Medical Centre, Harvard Medical School, Boston, Massachusetts 02115, also Microbiology Department – Unit of Arizona, Bio-medical U.S. Army Aberdeen Proving Ground, Maryland 21010.
(*Conclusion*: OPs do cause long-term effects in primates and more work must be done on this.)

M.K. Johnson: *Delayed Neuropathy caused by some organophosphorus esters – Mechanism and Challenge*, Biochemical MRC, Toxicology Unit, Carshalton.

The effects of pesticides on human health, Volume III. Appendices of minutes of evidence order by House of Commons, HMSO (12 May 1987).

John L. Laseter, William J. Rea, R. Ildefonso, B.S. Deleon, Joel R. Buther: *Clinical Ecology*, Vol. II, No. 1 (Autumn, 1984).
(*Abstract*: Using high resolution gas chromatography and high resolution Mass Spec. used to qualitatively and quantitatively characterize 16 different synthetic chlorinated hydrocarbon pesticides and common metabolites present in randomly selected environmentally sensitive patients. 200 initially screened; 99 per cent had residues at or above 0.05 parts per billion level in their sera. Data suggests chlorinated hydrocarbon pesticides are extremely common in the patient population investigated.)

B.J. Dowhy, J.L. Laseter and J. Storer: 'The transplacental migration

and accumulation in blood of volatile organic constituents' – *Paediat. Res.* – 10 – 696 – 701 (1976). University of New Orleans, Department of Biological Sciences, New Orleans, Louisiana USA; Charity Hospital of Louisana, New Orleans, Louisiana, USA.
(*Extract*: Gas chromatographic-mass spectrometric analysis of profiles of low molecular weight volatile organic constituents obtained from cord blood and maternal blood samples collected at birth reflect transplacentally acquired compounds. The transplacental passage of halogenated hydrocarbons, plastic components, and abnormal accumulations of compounds have been demonstrated. In the 11 paired cord blood-maternal blood samples analyzed, the relative amounts of constituents in cord blood closely correspond to those quantities present in the maternal blood. However, some of the over 100 components are present in the cord blood in significantly higher concentrations than in the maternal blood, suggesting a possible selective one-way transfer of certain constituents into the fetus. Benzene, carbon tetrachloride, and chloroform are present in quantities equal to or greater than in maternal blood. In one infant with a lumbosacral meningomyelocele abnormally high concentrations of acetone, other components and the food preservative 2,6-di-*tert*-butyl-4-methylphenol [BHT] were identified.)

J. Monro and R. Balarajan: Paper on sensitivity to pesticides in patients referred to the Department of Allergy and Environmental Medicine, Lister Hospital, London.

F.N. Kutz, Sc. Strassman and J.F. Sperling: Survey of selected organochlorine pesticides in the general population of the United States – Fiscal years 1970-1975. Ecological Monitoring Board TS – 768 United States Environmental Protection Agency, Washington DC 20460.
(*Overview*: Paper reports findings of selected OCs pesticide residues and their metabolites in human adipose tissue collected annually on a national basis from fiscal years 1970-1975.)

Lawrie Mott with the assistance of Martha Broad, *Pesticides in food – What the public need to know*, Natural Resources Defense Council Inc., San Francisco (15 March, 1984).
(*Overview*: Report where Natural Resources Defence Council (NRDC) raises concerns previously raised by congressional and governmental reports that federal and California pesticide regulatory

programmes did not sufficiently prevent public exposure to unsafe levels of pesticide residues in food. Although it is not statistically valid to derive definitive conclusions from the data obtained in the survey, it serves to corroborate earlier studies and demonstrates the need for major reforms in the regulatory procedures.)

Marcus Wassermann, Dora Wasserman, Similicas Cucos and Howard J. Millar: *World PCBs map storage and effects in man and his biologic environment in the 70s.* Department of Occupational Health, Hebrew University, Hadassah Medical School, Jerusalem, Israel.
(*Outline*: Surveys 15 areas of the world. Map of mercury, lead, and arsenic levels in humans. Article entitled: 'Indian pesticide disaster fuels fears over UK food chemical laws'. *Journal of Alternative Medicine*, January 1988.)
(*Overview*: Background information to the issue of pesticides, p. 2.)

Thomas A. Gossal, J. Douglas Bricker: *Principles of clinical toxicology,* Chapter 9 – Pesticides, pp. 128-152.

J. Telch and D.H. Jarvis: 'Acute intoxication with lindane (gamma benzene hexachloride)', *CMA Journal 126,* pp. 662-663 (1982).

H.R. Wolfe, W.F. Durham and J.F. Armstrong: 'Exposure of workers to pesticides', Arch. – Environ. Health – 14, pp. 622-663.

Edited by D.M. Conning and A.B.G. Lansdown, *Toxic hazards in food,* pp. 136-138.

Hepatucellular adaptation and injury – structural and biochemical changes following Dieldrin and Dimethylbutter yellow. Lab. Investigation (1969).

Fd. Cosmet, A.E.J. McGill and J.A. Robinson: *Organochlorine insecticide residues in complete prepared meals* – a 12-month survey in S.E. England.

Fd. Cosmet – Toxicol II, A.I.T. Walker, E. Thorpe, D.E. Stevenson, *The toxicology of dieldrin* (HEOD). I. long-term oral toxicity studies in mice, pp. 415-432 (1973).

IARC – Monographs on the evaluation of the carcinogenic risk of chemicals to man – some organochlorine pesticides, IARC Lyon, Vol. 5 (1974).

Occurrence of chlorinated phenoxy acid herbicides and chlorinated phenols in environmentally sensitive patients. Presented to the American Academy of Environmental Medicine (1955).

Analysis and distribution of selected volatile organics in whole blood from environmentally sensitive patients. Presented to the American Academy of Environmental Medicine (1985).

W.J. Rea, E.J. Fenyves, A.R. Johnson, R.E. Smily and D.E. Sprague: *A double blind study of chemical sensitivity* (1981).

Pesticides in agricultural run-off and their effects on downstream water quality. Environmental Toxicology and Chemistry (4), pp. 267-279 (1982).

C.E. McKane and R.J. Hance: 'Determination of residue of 2,4,5-T in soil by gas chromatography of the n-butyl esters'. *J. Chromatogr.,* 69, 204-206 (1972).

A.S.Y. Chau and K.J. Terry, Assn. Offic., *Analysis of Pesticides by Chemical Derivitisation pt III Gas chromatographic characteristics and conditions for the formation of pentafluorabenzl derivatives of ten herbicidal acids.* Analytical Chemists, 59, p. 633 (1976).

Letter to *Farmers Weekly* entitled 'Stress more like poisoning' (25 September, 1987).
(*Overview:* Stress in farming not due to money and other everyday problems but to exposure to pesticides and sheep dip.)

MAFF: *Report of the Working Party on Pesticide Residues 1982-1985,* Food Surveillance Paper No. 16, HMSO.

Davidson and Passmore: *Human Nutrition and Dietetics* (Church Livingstone, 1987).

Peter Snell: *Pesticide Residues and Food* (London Food Commission, 1986).

Nigel Dudley: *Nitrates in Food and Water* (London Food Commission, 1986).

McCance and Widdowson: *The Composition of Foods* (HMSO, 1978).

Shelter's Housing Magazine *Roof,* May-June 1987. Copies are obtainable from 88 Old Street, London EC1V 9HU. Article on spraying for woodworm in the home.

'Chlorinated insecticides in body fat of people in United States'. *Science* pp. 142-593 (1963).

W.S. Hoffman and W.I. Fishbein: *Pesticide storage in human fat tissue, JAMA*, pp. 188-819 (1 June 1964).

Mark S. Gibson, M.D., V. Gary Hoss, M.D., John L. Laseter, William J. Rea. *Physicians' Clinical Guide 1987 Edition*. Case Study Information – Environmental Health Information Centre, 990 N. Bowser Road, Suite 800, Richardson, Texas 75081.

R.D. De Laune, R.P. Gambrell and K.S. Reddy: 'Fate of pentachlorophenol in estuarine sediment'.
(*Abstract*: The fate of PCP following major spill in a Louisiana Gulf estuary was examined. Degradation of PCP was strongly influenced by sediment pH and oxidation-reduction potential conditions. Degradation rates decreased with decreasing sediment oxidation-reduction potential. Maximum degradation occurred at pH 8.00 absorption. Description studies show PCP to be more tightly bound to oxidized sediment than to reduced sediment. The measured degradation rates suggest that microbal degradation could acount for the observed disappearance of residual PCP in the spill area.)

Environmental Pollution Series B6, pp. 297-308 (1983).
Lab. for Wetland Soils and Sediments, Centre for Wetland Resources, Louisiana State University, Baton Rouge, Louisiana 70803-7511, USA.

Further reading: J. Cook and C. Kaufman: *Portrait of Poison. The 2,4,5-T story* (Pluto Press, 1982).

Further reading: Council on Environmental Quality and the Environment and the Department of State 1982 – The Global 2000 Report to the President (Penguin).

Further reading: S. George: *How the other half dies* (Penguin, 1976).

GIFAP International Group of National Associations of Pesticide Manufacturers 1985. *Pesticide Residues in Food*, GIFAP, Avenue Hamoir 12, 1180 Brussels.

M.B. Green, A.S. Hartley and T.F. West: *Chemicals for crop protection and pest control* (Pergamon Press, Oxford, 1977).

K.A. Hassall: *The Chemistry of Pesticides* (Macmillan, 1985).

The Food and Environment Protection Act (HMSO, 1985).

R.F. Luck, R. Van den Bosch and R. Garica: 'Chemical insect control a troubled pest management strategy'. *Bio. Science* 27.

F. Matsumara: *Toxicology of Insecticides* (Plenum Press, New York, 1975).

Pesticide usage. Preliminary Report 41 Review of usage of pesticides in Agriculture and Horticulture in England and Wales 1980-1983 (MAFF, London, 1985).

Steering group of food surveillance, Ninth Report – Report of the Working Party on Pesticide Residues (HMSO, London, 1982-1985).

Pall of Poison – the Spray Drift Problem. Soil Association, Walnut Tree Manor, Haughley, Stowmarket, Suffolk (1984).

R. Van den Bosch: *The pesticide conspiracy* (Prism Press, Dorset, 1978).

Long-term hazards to man from man-made chemicals in the environment (1978) quoted in Royal Society – criticizes routine toxicity tests *Nature,* 274, p. 413 (1978).

The Royal College of Veterinary Surgeons – Personal communication (February 1987).

The Observer – 26 April 1987: 'Poisonous spray incidents ignored by inspectors', by Geoffrey Lean, Environment Correspondent.

J.A.R. Bates and S. Gorbach: 'Recommended approach to the appraisal of risks to consumers from pesticide residues in crops and food commodities'. *Pure and Appl. Chem.,* Vol. 59, No. 4, pp. 611-624 (1987).

Parkinson's disease

J.W. Langston: 'MPTP and Parkinson's Disease'. Reprinted from *Trends in Neuro Sciences,* Vol. 8, No. 2, pp. 79-83 (February, 1985).

A. Barbeau: 'Etiology of Parkinson's Disease: A Research Strategy'. *Canadian Journal of Neurological Sciences,* Vol. II, No. 1, pp. 24-28 (February, 1984).

A. Barbeau: *The relative roles of ageing, genetic susceptibility and*

204   *The Residue Report*

environment in Parkinson's disease (The United Parkinson Foundation, May 1985).

A. Barbeau, M. Roy and T. Cloutier: 'Smoking, Cancer and Parkinson's Disease'. *Annals of Neurology*, Vol. 20, No. 1 (July, 1986).

J.W. Langston, I. Irwin and G.A. Ricaurte: *Neurotoxins, Parkinsonism and Parkinson's Disease in Pharmacology and Therapeutics* (Special Issue: Parkinsonism), D.B. Clane (Ed.) (Pergamon Press, 19--).

Parkinson Newsletter, No. 57, May 1986. Published by The Parkinson's Disease Society, 36 Portland Place, London W1N 3DG (Tel: 01-323 1174).

BBC *Horizon* programme: *The Frozen Addict* (7 April, 1987).
(*Overview*: The programme described how a group of drug addicts who had been exposed to a chemical similar to a herbicide experienced the effects which resembled instant Parkinsonism. As the symptoms baffled the doctors, the addicts were then given treatment as if they had Parkinson's disease and temporarily recovered. It is hoped that through this unfortunate event some positive new breakthroughs may come in the etiology of Parkinson's disease.)

Georgina Ferry: 'New light on Parkinson's disease'. *New Scientist* (5 February, 1987).

Aluminium

H. Tomlinson and L.N. Fowler: *Aluminium Utensils and Disease* (1958).

Professor J.A. Edwardson, MRC. *Aluminium and Alzheimer's disease* (April, 1987). Neuroendocrinology Unit, Newcastle General Hospital, Westgate Road, Newcastle upon Tyne NE4 6BE (Tel: 091-273 251). Many important studies on these topics are in progress at the moment. If you would like to receive an update of these notes in the future, write to Professor Edwardson at the above address. Meanwhile, further information on this topic can be found in the following references:

M.M. Candy, et al: 'Aluminosilicates and senile plaque formation in Alzheimer's disease'. *The Lancet 1*, pp. 354-357 (1986).

D.R. Crapper McLachlan and B.J. Farnell: 'Aluminium and neuronal degeneration'. In *Metal Ions in Neurology and Psychiatry*. S. Gabay, J. Harris and B.T. Ho (eds.), pp. 69-87 (Alan R. Liss, Inc. New York, 1985).

J.A. Edwardson et al: 'Aluminosilicates and the ageing brain: implications for the pathogenesis of Alzheimer's disease'. In *Silicon Biochemistry*. Wiley, Chichester, pp. 160-179 (Ciba Foundation Symposium 121, 1986).

P.O. Ganrot: 'Metabolism and possible health effects of aluminium'. *Environmental Health Perspectives*, 65, pp. 363-441 (1986). (The most comprehensive recent review.)

D. Perl and A.R. Brody: 'Alzheimer's disease: X-ray spectrometric evidence of aluminium accumulation in neurofibrillary tangle-bearing neurones'. *Science*, 208, pp. 297-299 (1980).

K. Tennakone and S. Wickramanayake: 'Aluminium leaching from cooking utensils'. *Nature*, 325, p. 202 (1987).

T. Vogt: *Water quality and health: a study of possible relationships between aluminium in drinking water and dementia*. Social and Economic Study No. 61 from the Central Bureau of Statistics, Oslo (in Norwegian) (1986).

Philip J. Hills: *Washington Post Service* (Researchers Report Clue to Alzheimers, 1987).

Neville Hodgkinson: *Trouble bubbles on the burner*, Medicum p. 29 (1987).

Janet Watts: 'The challenge of senile dementia'. *The Observer* (1987).

Nitrates

D. Hodges: *Agriculture, Nitrates and Health*, Soil Association Quarterly report (1985).

H.H. Koepf: 'Nitrate – an ailing organism call for health'. *Biodynamics*, No. 73 (1965).

Leonard A. Cohen: 'Cancer and Diet'. *Scientific American*, Vol. 257, No. 5 (September, 1987).
Recommendations aimed at reducing the incidence of cancers associated with nutrition are based on limited but suggestive evidence from epidemiological studies and animal experiments.

Accumulation of nitrates, National Acid Sciences Agriculture Board – Washington, D.C., ISBN 0-309-02038-7 (1972).

A.M. Walters: *Nitrates in water, soil, plants and animals*, International Journal. Environmental Studies, pp. 5-105 (1973).

Taylor: 'Nitrates, Nitrites, Nitrosamines and Cancer'. *Nutrition and Health*, 2, p. 47.

C. Aubert: 'Les nitrates dans les legumes'. *Nature et Progrès* 76, p. 18 (1982).

A.M. Walters: *Nitrates in water, soil, plants and animals*, International *Estimation by HPLC*. Science Department, Farnborough College of Technology, Hampshire.

Nutrition and Health, Vol. 4, pp. 141-149 (1986).
(*Abstract*: Over the past 50 years the development of high tech farming has led to excessive amounts of fertilizer being applied to the soil. Some research aspects of this abuse are described in relation to the uptake of nitrate into vegetables. In order to monitor this problem a high precision HPLC method capable of rapid through put has evolved. Using this HPLC method the results over a 12-month period are presented and compared with the existing standards now legally enforced in Switzerland and Holland.)

John R. Fletcher, Sylvia Low and A.M. Walters: *Effect of cookery on the nitrate levels in vegetables*. Department of Science, Farnborough College of Technology, Farnborough, Hampshire GU14 6SB.
(*Abstract*: Effects on the nitrate content of vegetables exposed to boiling in water for various lengths of time is described. Some varieties show a steady decrease in nitrate levels, others an initial rise. The nitrate content of the cooking water used shows a sustained increase as the cooking time is extended.)

A.M. Walters: *J. Soil Assoc.*, 16, p. 149 (1970).

A.M. Walters: *International Journal Environ. Studies*, 5, p. 105 (1973).

Wooten Buckle: *J. Sc. Food Agriculture*, 36, p. 297 (1985).

Walters, Fletcher, Law: *Nutrition and Health*, 4, 3, p. 141 (1986).

Taylor: *Nutrition and Health*, 2, p. 47 (1983).

Walters: *The Environmentalist*, 3, 3, p. 219 (1983).

Walters: *The Ecologist*, 15, 4, p. 189 (1983).

Fred Pearce: 'The hills are alive with nitrates', *New Scientist* (10 December, 1987).
(*Abstract*: An overview of the situation, bringing together all aspects of the problem, especially important are the examples of gross pollution, and the failure of the Environment Secretary to understand the whole issue.)

Geoffrey Cannon: 'Water – is it driving us mad?', *Sunday Telegraph Magazine* (March, 1988).

'The pesticide content of surface water draining from agricultural fields – a review'. *Journal of Environment Quality*, 7 (4), pp. 459-472 (1978).

Guidelines for drinking water quality, Volume 1, World Health Organization (Geneva, 1984).

Summary Report. *Drinking Water and Health*, National Academy of Sciences, Washington D.C. (1977).

B.T. Croll: *The effects of the agricultural use of herbicides on fresh waters*, Anglian Water Paper 13 given at a Water Research Centre Conference in conjunction with the WHO.

Trends in nitrate concentrations in English rivers and fertiliser use, Water Treatment Examination, 19, pp. 277-288 (1970).

Nitrates in Water, A nitrate co-ordination group, HMSO, ISBN: 0-117-51866-2. Pollution paper No. 26 (1986).

The rising tide of nitrate pollution – to prevent or cure? ENDS Report 97, pp. 9-12 (February, 1983).

Decision soon on nitrates, ENDS Report, Report No. 120 (1985).

Nitrate and water resources with particular reference to groundwater, Central Water Planning Unit (1977) Reading Bridge Road, Reading RG1 8PS.

B. Singh and G.S. Sekhom: 'Nitrate pollution of groundwater from farm use of nitrogen fertiliser', a review, *Agriculture and Environment*, 4(3), pp. 207-225 (1978).

H. Shuval and N. Gruebler: *Infant methamoglobinemia and other health effects on nitrates in drinking water*. Proc IAWPR Conference Nitrogen as a Water Pollutant (Copenhagen, 1975).

S.R. Tannenbaum, et al: 'Nitrite in human saliva and its possible relationship to nitrosamine formation', *J. Natl. Cancer Institute*, 53, p. 79 (1974).

David Forman, Samin Al Dabbagh and Richard Dell: 'Nitrates, nitrites and gastric cancer in Great Britain', *Nature*, 313, pp. 620-628 (1985).

'The health effects of nitrate, nitrites and N-nitroso compounds', National Academy of Sciences, Washington DC (1981).

Nitrates, Nitrites and N-nitroso compounds, Environmental Health Criteria 5, World Health Organization (Geneva, 1977).

D.G. Miller: *Nitrates in drinking water*, Water Research Council External Report 9-M/2 Medmenham (1982).

Packaging materials

'Volatile nitrosamines in cured meat packaged in elastic rubber netting', *Journal of Agriculture and Food Chemistry* (1987).

'What cling film puts into your food', *New Scientist* (14 August, 1986).

'Don't use cling film in cooking', *Which* (December, 1986).

Residues of dental origin

M.J. Vimy and F.L. Lorscheider: 'Intra-oral air mercury released from dental amalgam', *J. Dent. Res.* 64(8), pp. 1069-1071 (1985a).

Sames authors as above: 'Serial measurement of intra-oral mercury:

Estimation of daily dose from amalgam'. *J. Dent. Res.* 64, pp. 1072-1075 (1985b).

D.D. Gay, R.D. Cox and J.W. Reinhardt: Letter: 'Chewing releases mercury from fillings', *Lancet* 1(8123), pp. 985-986 (1979).

C.W. Svare, et al: 'The effect of dental amalgams on mercury levels in expired air.' *J. Dent. Res.* 60, pp. 1668-1671 (1981).

U. Traugott, E.L. Reinherz and C.S. Raine: 'Multiple Sclerosis: Distribution of T cell subsets with active chronic lesions'. *Science* 219, p. 308 (1983).

G. Stingl, L.A. Gazze, N. Czarnecki and K. Wolff: 'T cell abnormalities in atopic dermatites patients: Imbalances in T cell subpopulations.' *J. Invest. Dermatology* 76, p. 468 (1981).

L. Chatenoud and M.A. Bach: 'Abnormalities of T cell subsets in glomerulonephritis and systemic lupus erythematosus'. *Kidney. Int.* 20, p. 267 (1981).

D.Y. Leung, A.R. Rhodes and R.S. Geha: 'Enumeration of T cell subsets of atopic dermatitis using monoclonal antibodies'. *Journal of Allergy Clin. Immunol.* 67, p. 450 (1981).

M. Butler, D. Atherton and R.J. Levinsky: 'Qualitative and functional deficit of suppressor T cells in children with atopic excema', *Clin. Exp. Immunol.* 50, p. 92 (1982).

Reinherz et al: 'Loss of supressor T cells in active Multiple Sclerosis', *N. Engl. J. Med.* 303, p. 125 (1980).

C. Morimoto et al: 'Alterations in immunoregulatory T cell subsets in active SLE', *J. Clin. Invest.* 66, p. 1171 (1980).

P.F. Kohler and J. Vaughn: 'The autoimmune diseases', *J. AM Med. Assoc.* 248, p. 2446 (1982).

D.W. Eggleston: 'Effect of dental amalgam and nickel alloys on T lymphocytes: preliminary report', *J. Prosthetic Dentistry* 5151, 5, pp. 617-623 (1984).

International Academy of Oral Medicine and Toxicology, New York, (November 1986).

Sam Ziff: *The Toxic Time Bomb* (Thorsons, 1986).

R. Schiele et al: 'Studies on the mercury content in brain and kidney related to number and condition of amalgam fillings'. Institution of Occupational and Social Medicine, University of Erlangen, Nurnberg, West Germany. Presented at the Amalgam – Viewpoints from medicine and dental medicine symposium, 12 March, Cologne, West Germany (1984).

L. Friberg, L. Kullman, B. Lind, M. Nylander: 'Mercury and the central nervous system in relation to amalgam fillings', *Lakartidningen* 83, pp. 519-22 (1986).

David W. Eggleston and Magnus Nylander: 'Correlation of dental amalgam with mercury in brain tissue'. The *J. Pros. Dent.* pp. 704-6 (December, 1987).

H. Freden, L. Hellden, P. Millending: 'Mercury content in gingival tissues adjacent to amalgam fillings'. *Odont Review* 25, 2, pp. 207-10 (1974).

P.R. Goldschmidt, R.B. Cogen, S.B. Taubman: 'Effects of amalgam corrosion products on human cells'. *J. Periodont. Res.* 11, 2, pp. 108-115 (1976).

P. Stortbecker: 'Mercury poisoning from dental amalgam – a hazard to the human brain', Stortbecker Foundation Akerbyvagen 282, S-183 p. 35 Taby, Stockholm, Sweden.

'Hazards in Dentistry – The Mercury Debate', British Dental Society for Clinical Nutrition, Conference 1984, at Kings' College, Cambridge (July 1985).

Djerassi and Berova: 'The possibility of allergic reactions from silver amalgam restorations', *Int. Dent. J.* 19(4), pp. 481-488 (1969).

It's All in Your Head, Dr Hal Huggins, 1985.

E.G. Miller, W.L. Perry and M.J. Wagner: 'Prevalence of mercury hypersensitivity in dental students', *J. Dent. Res.*, 64 Special Issue Abstracts page 388 (March 1985).

Nebenfurrerl et al: 'Mercury Allergy in Budapest', *Contact Dermatitis* 10(2), pp. 121-122 (1984).

'Biocompatability of Dental Materials', NIDR/ADA workshop (Chicago, 13 July, 1984).

The food chain connection

'Organochlorine pesticides and polychlorinated biphenyls in livers of cod from Southern Baltic 1983'. Taken from *Nutrition Abstracts and Reviews* Series A, Volume 57, No. 10 (October 1987).
(*Conclusion*: Livers of cod caught in the Baltic were considered unsuitable for human consumption.)

Average total dietary intake of OC compounds from the Finnish diet.
(*Abstract*: The main source was found in fish giving an overall 28 per cent – the most significant concentration in one type of fish was in the Baltic herring which gave 70 per cent. The OC's most abundant were P.C.B. and D.D.T.)

Moilanen, Pyysalo and Kumpulainen, *Nutritional Abstracts and Reviews* Series A, Human and Experimental, Volume 57, No. 10 (October 1987).

J.H. Petersen and K.G. Jensen: *Pesticide residues in black tea*, National Food Agency, Morkhoj Bygade, Soborg, Denmark (1987).
(*Conclusion*: Pesticides were found to be present – but it was estimated that the levels were safe.)

Margarine, butter, honey and vegetable oils as sources of OC compounds in the Finnish diet. The oils included 1) Rapeseed 2) Sunflower 3) Soya bean 4) Turnip rape oils by R. Moilanen, J. Kumpulainen, H. Pyysalo *Nutritional Abstracts and Reviews*, Series A, Human and Experimental, Volume 57, No. 10 (October 1987).
(*Conclusion*: OCs were found to be present in all foods, but the levels were considered to be within WHO values.)

'Herbicidal residues in Aquatic Environments' in *Advances in Chemistry* Series III. Fate of organic pesticides in the aquatic environment. D. Faust (Ed.), American Chemical Society, Washington, D.C. (1972).

Further reading: 'Freshwater Fisherines Laboratory Faskally'. Pitlochry, Scotland by A.V. Holden.

Morlais Owens: *Some aspects of the chemicals and pesticide pollution of inland waters*. Water Pollution Research Laboratory of the Department of the Environment, Stevenage, Herts.

Organochlorine insecticides in water Part I – Water treatment examination, 18, pp. 255-274 (1969).

Organochlorine insecticides in water Part II – Water treatment examination, 18, pp. 275-287 (1969).

Residues in cow's milk

M. O'Keeffe, J.F. Eades, K.L. Strickland and D. Harrington: 'Crufomate residues in milk and milk products following treatment of dairy cows for warble fly' in *Journal of the Science of Food and Agriculture* Vol. 33 (1982).

M. O'Keeffe, J.F. Eades and K.L. Strickland: 'Fenthion residues in milk and milk products, following treatment of dairy cows for warble fly' in *Journal of the Science of Food and Agriculture* (1978).

M. O'Keeffe, J.F. Eades and K.L Strickland: 'Phosmet residues in milk following treatment of dairy cows for warble fly', *J. Sci. Food Agric.* Vol 34, pp. 463-465 (1983).

J.L. Greger: 'Aluminium content of the American diet', *Food Technology* (May, 1985).

Potato Marketing Board – personal communication.

Organics in action

Further reading: L.D. Hills: *A Month-by-Month Guide to Organic Gardening* (Thorsons, 1983).

Organic foods

' "Real meat" could be the future growth area' – *Meat Trade Journal* (25 April, 1985).

Further reading: Orville Schell: *Modern Meat – Antibiotics, Hormones and the Pharmaceutical Farm*. ISBN 0-394-51890-X.

The ecology lifestyle

W.J. Rea: 'Controlled environment for study of environmental pollutants in buildings' (1981).

W.J. Rea, R.E. Smiley, D.E. Sprague, A.R. Johnson, A.L. de Victoria, W.F. Tucker and E.J. Fenyves: 'Chemical sensitivity as a result of over exposure in the work place'.

W.J. Rea, R.E. Smiley, D.E. Sprague, A.R. Johnson, A.L. de Victoria, W.F. Tucker and E.J. Fenyves: 'Formaldehyde sensitivity following exposure to building material'.

John Seymour and Herbert Girardet: *Blueprint for a Green Planet* (Dorling Kindersley 1987).

Friends of the Earth Handbook (Macdonald, 1987).

Feeding babies and young children

Mes, Jos and Pui-Yan Lau: 'Distribution of Polychlorinated Biphenyl Congeners in Human Milk and Blood During Lactation', *Bulletin of Environmental Contamination and Toxicology*, Vol. 31, pp. 639-643 (1983).

Kim Wickstrom, Heikki Pyysalo and Martti A. Siimes: 'Levels of Chlordane Hexachlorobenzene, PCB and DDT Compounds in Finnish Human Milk in 1982', *Bulletin of Environmental Contamination and Toxicology*, Vol. 31, pp. 251-256 (1983).

B.L. Mirkin: 'Diphenylhydantoin: Placental transport, fetal localization, neonatal metabolism and possible teratogenic effects', *Pediat. Pharmacol. Ther.*, 78(2) p. 329 (1971).

R.R. Monson, L. Rosenberg, S.C. Hartz, S. Shapito, P.O. Heinonen and D. Slone: 'Diphenylhydantoin and selected congenital malformations', *N. Engl. J. Med.* 289(20), p. 1049 (1973).

S. Beardall: 'Today's children fatter, sicker and more disturbed', *The Times* (11 September, 1985).

'Organochlorine contaminants in human milk', Chemistry Department, University Benin, Benin City, Nigeria, taken from *Nutrition*

Abstracts and Reviews, Series A, Human and Experimental, Vol. 37, No. 10 (October, 1987).

'Spray drift blamed for pall of poison', *Laboratory News* – news journal to the scientific industry, 40 The Boulevard, Crawley, W. Sussex RH10 1XD; Editorial Department: 0293 547474.

(*Quote*: Health experts expressing concern that the human reproductive process could be affected by present levels of exposure to toxic chemicals, mainly pesticides.)

Hypothesis concerning Sudden Infant Death Syndrome (SIDS)

C. Pheiffer: 'Zinc and other micro-nutrients', Ch3 Pub. Inc. (1978).

Select Committee on Nutrition and Human Needs, U.S. Senate, 1977, 1980 up-date mental health and mental development.

D.V. Roberts: *Pharmacology and toxicology of organophosphorus pesticides*. 'Campaign for pesticide-free food'. *The Lancet* (13 April, 1985).

M.K. Johnson: 'The delayed neuropathy caused by some organo-phosphorus esters – mechanism and challenge', MRC Laboratory (Carshalton, 1975).

A. Andrews: *Abnormal reactions and their frequency in cattle following the use of OPs warble fly dressing*, VET Department, pp. 109, 171, 175 (Bletchley, 1981).

P. Duffy, J. Burchfiel, P. Bartels, M. Gaon, Van N. Sim: 'Long term effects of an OP upon the human electroencephalogram', *Tox. & Appl. Pharm.*, p. 47 (1979).

D. Hubbard and A. Riopelle: 'Prenatal manganese deprivation and early behaviour of primates', *JOP* Vol. 6, No. 4.

D. Oberleas, D. Caldwell, A. Prasaa: 'Trace Elements and Behaviour' *Int. Review of Neurobiology* (1972).

'Congenital pancytopenia association with multiple congenital anomalies' (Fanconi type), *Pediatrics*, pp. 15-325 (1955).

R. McDonald and B. Goldschmidt: 'Pancytopenia with congenital defects' (Fanconi's anaemia), *Arch. Dis. Child*, pp. 35-367 (1960).

L.R. Nilsson: 'Chronic pancytopenia with multiple congenital abnormalities', *Acta. Paediat.*, pp. 49-518 (1960).

E.B. Adams: 'Aplastic anaemia: Review of 27 cases', *The Lancet* 1, p. 657 (1951).

T.H. Boon, J.N. Walton: 'Aplastic anaemia', *Quart. J. Med.* 20 p. 75 (1951).

Report of the consultative council on congenital abnormality in the Yarram District, Department of Primary Industry, Canberra, Victoria, Australia (1978).

Report on assessment of a field investigation of 6-year spontaneous abortion rates in three Oregon areas in relation to forest 2,4,5-T spray practices. (E.P.A., 1979).

'Children healthier 35 years ago', *The Guardian* (10 September, 1985).

'The milk of human blindness', *The Guardian* (4 April, 1987). Amongst other questions asks whether P.C.B.'s are crossing the placenta and concentrating in human milk.

Watchdog without teeth

R.S. Nicholson, 'Surveys of pesticide residues in food 1983', *J. Assoc. Publ. Analysts*, 22, pp. 51-57 (1984).

Policy Statement 1985 - Handbook. Prepared by the Association of Public Analysts.

Index

E FOR ADDITIVES

The Best-selling, award-winning definitive E number guide

Maurice Hanssen with Jill Marsden

Cracks the 'E' number code and enables you to understand the lists of additives that appear on the packs of the food you buy, so that you can see exactly what has been added, where it comes from, why it has been added, what it does to the food and — if anything — what it might do to you.

Here is all you need to know about:

- Which additives are natural and which can have harmful effects.
- The reasons behind the use of preservatives, colours and flavourings in our foods.
- How to make informed choices when you shop.
- Additives in wine and vitamin supplements.
- Additives in meat.
- Guidelines on acceptable daily intake.

This vital guide has led a consumer revolution, causing the food industry to re-think its policy on additives. No one who is concerned with the quality of the food they eat can afford to be without this invaluable reference book.

FOOD IRRADIATION: THE FACTS

Tony Webb and Dr Tim Lang
of the London Food Commission

Food irradition: its supporters say it could revolutionize the way we eat. Food would stay edible for longer, prepared meals could sit on the larder shelf for months before being popped in the microwave for an instant hot dinner.

   Food irradiation: its detractors say it could result in unidentifiable poisons remaining in seemingly 'fresh' food, and the potential for illegal abuse of irradiation to disguise decay could result in food poisoning and even death.

   What do you, the consumer, know about food irradiation? Is the issue clouded with fears of nuclear fallout? Or are you confident the authorities will ensure our food is safe to eat? Here at last is clear, concise information that has been assembled by the close monitoring of the development of food irradiation. Here are the facts on an issue that affects us all, explained by experts whose main concern is for you, the consumer. Here is all the evidence you need to make an informed decision about the treatment of the food we eat.

HAPPINESS IS JUNK-FREE FOOD

Fight Hyperactivity and Other Food Allergies with Quick and Easy Healthy Meals for All the Family

Janet Ash and Dulcie Roberts

Taking the slogan of the Hyperactive Children's Support Group as their title, two mothers have compiled this long-awaited recipe and reference book which will be welcomed by parents of hyperactive children — and indeed by all allergy victims — everywhere.

Here is a wide range of dishes to suit all occasions which will be enjoyed by all the family, and which are not only tasty and economical but are also — most importantly — free from all artificial colourings, flavourings and preservatives. The recipes also exclude certain fruits and vegetables that contain salicylates — natural substances to which many hyperactive children are sensitive. Not only that, many recipes are also suitable for other allergy sufferers by being grain-free, gluten-free, milk-free or egg-free. Each recipe is accompanied by an at-a-glance guide to show if it is right for you.

A wealth of handy hints, gleaned from the authors' own experience, plus useful addresses and other resources, are included to help you gain as much practical help as possible from this invaluable handbook.